Conversations

On

The Books of

Leviticus and Numbers

By

Danny Glenn Thomas

Just for the Basic Series

Copyright 2020 By Danny G. Thomas

Table of Contents

Foreword

Paul tells Timothy in **2 Timothy 2:15:** *"Be diligent to present yourself approved to God, a worker who does not need to be ashamed, rightly dividing the word of truth."* **NKJV**. The **King James Version** renders this verse: *"Study to show thyself approved unto God, a workman that needeth not to be ashamed, rightly dividing the word of truth."* The **New Living Translation** has stated it this way: *"Work hard so you can present yourself to God and receive his approval. Be a good worker, one who does not need to be ashamed and who correctly explains the word of truth."* Eugene Peterson in his paraphrase, **The Message,** writes: *"Concentrate on doing your best for God, work you won't be ashamed of, laying out the truth plain and simple."*

This is what I have set out to do. I am presenting a plain, simple, and basic commentary on the Word of God. I want to present the Word, compared by the Word, with the hope of creating a greater desire of the reader to want to know more and to seek to go deeper into God's Word.

I found written in the front of my Dad's first preaching Bible this statement: *"The task of the scholar is to guarantee the purity of the text; to get as close as possible to the Word as originally given. He may compare Scripture with Scripture until he discovers the true meaning of the text. But right there, his authority ends. He must never sit in judgment upon what is written; he must not bring the meaning of the Word before the bar of his reason."* I do not know the source of this statement, but it is true, and that is my desire as I write this series of commentaries or expositions on Scripture.

Introduction to Leviticus

The book of Leviticus encourages the believer to come into the holiness of God as we worship Him. *Coram Deo*: "in the presence of God." God is holy and those who worship Him must worship Him in Holiness and truth.

God is also a Spirit and those who worship Him, Jesus told the woman at the well, must worship Him in spirit and truth. **John 4:24:** *"God is Spirit, and those who worship Him must worship in spirit and truth."* **NKJV**.

Worship is not a casual thing; it is a holy thing. It is not a Sunday thing; it is an everyday thing. Worship is a *"set-apart"* thing or a set time thing. We prepare for worship, though all that we do in life must be done as though we were doing it unto the Lord, as we read in **1 Corinthians 10:31**.

The whole life of a believer is to be lived for the glory of God! God is not our buddy. He is our Creator, our holy God Almighty.

If we think otherwise, perhaps we should rethink upon what worship is: *"And so, dear brothers and sisters, I plead with you to give your bodies to God. Let them be a living and holy sacrifice—the kind he will accept. When you think of what he has done for you, is this too much to ask? Don't copy the behavior and customs of this world, but let God transform you into a new person by changing the way you think. Then you will know what God wants you to do, and you will know how good and pleasing and perfect his will really is."* **Romans 12:1 & 2 NLT**

Leviticus gives to the believer God's idea of worship:

- What God desires of him in worship,
- How he is to serve God in life,

- How he is to obey God in life.

The key verse of Leviticus is **Leviticus 11:44:** *"I am the Lord your God. You shall therefore consecrate yourselves, and you shall be holy; for I am holy. . . ."* **NKJV**. Also found in **Leviticus 19:2**.

The Levites are the descendants of Levi, of the tribe of Levi, and they were charged with the care of the Tabernacle and worship. They were not given a section of land as the other tribes were, because they were to be given to the Lord.

Chapter 1

Burnt Offerings

The book of Leviticus begins by covering the five offerings associated with worship at the Tabernacle. Those five offerings are:

1. The **Burnt Offering** which was *voluntary* for the individual person; and it was an offering for sins that he has committed. However the Burnt Offering was mandatory for <u>the sins of the nation of Israel</u>. The priest would offer a Burnt Offering every Sabbath, once a month, and at the feast days.

2. The **Grain Offering**, sometimes called the **Drink Offering**, was also *voluntary*; and the purpose for this offering was to express devotion to God. It was a less expensive offering in that it did not require blood.

3. The **Peace Offering** was also *voluntary*; and its purpose was thanksgiving to God for the blessings that He had given to them. This offering was the only offering that was shared with others. The Peace Offering reminds me of our holiday, Thanksgiving. Included in this offering was a <u>Wave Offering</u> and a <u>Heave Offering</u>. The Peace Offering expressed a commitment to God.

4. The **Sin Offering** was a mandatory offering. The purpose for this offering was for the purification of a person.

5. The **Trespass Offering,** or **Guilt Offering,** was a mandatory offering. The purpose for this offering was for justification before God.

There is always a procedure that was taken in the blood sacrifices. The animal, or bird must be spotless, and it must be dedicated to the Lord and acceptable by the Lord; and the sacrifice was given as a <u>substitute</u> for sin. As the priest placed his hands upon the sacrifice, it symbolized that the sacrifice was an acceptable one, and that it was a pleasing substitute before the Lord.

The required sacrifice for the Burnt Offering had to be a bull or oxen; a sheep or goat; a pigeon or turtledove. **Verses 3, 10 & 14**. These sacrifices varied in their value; and therefore any person could afford to make a sacrifice regardless of his circumstance, whether rich or poor.

The sacrifice must be killed, prepared, and then cleaned with water, by the priest. There were eight tables there, four on the north side of the courtyard and four on the south side of the courtyard.

The sacrifice must be butchered, or cut up by the priest in a specific way, and then laid upon the altar in a specific order. The blood of the animal or bird must sprinkled upon the base of the altar. **Verses 3 – 17**.

Just a note here, the courtyard was a very bloody place, and the work was very strenuous. The active priests who were doing the work of the Tabernacle must be between 25 and 50 years of age.

In **Numbers 4:2 – 4:** *"Take a census of the sons of Kohath from among the children of Levi, by their families, by their fathers' house, <u>from thirty years old and above</u>, <u>even to fifty years old</u>, all who enter the service to do the work in the tabernacle of meeting. This is the service of the sons of Kohath in the tabernacle of meeting, relating to the most holy things:"* **NKJV**. The strenuous work required in the sacrifice was one reason why the priests were to retire from the "hard work." **Numbers 8:23 – 26:** *"The Lord also instructed Moses, 'This is* *the rule the Levites must follow: They must begin serving in the Tabernacle <u>at the age of twenty-five</u>, and they <u>must retire at the age of fifty</u>. After retirement <u>they may assist</u> their fellow Levites by preforming guard duty at the Tabernacle, <u>but they may not officiate</u> in the service. This is how you will assign duties to the Levites."* **NLT**.

The most difficult part of officiating had to do with the slaughtering of the sacrifice animals and preparing them for being placed on the Altar of Burnt Offering.

An interesting notation is made in **Leviticus 3:16 & 17** concerning the offering process of sacrifice: *"and the priest shall burn them on the altar as food, an offering made by fire for a sweet aroma; <u>all the fat is the Lord's</u>. This shall be a perpetual statute throughout your generations in all <u>your dwellings: you shall eat neither fat nor blood</u>."* **NKJV**.

The fat is not to be eaten, because the fat is not good for your health. It is offered to the Lord alone: *"all the fat belongs to the Lord."* **Leviticus 3:16 NKJV**.

The acceptable sacrifice is a sweet aroma to God. In **Ephesians 5:2:** *"And walk in love, as Christ also has loved us and given Himself for us, an offering and a sacrifice to God for a sweet-smelling aroma."* **NKJV**.

In **Hebrews 10** we read that blood is required for almost all sacrifices: *"And according to the law almost all things are purified with blood, and <u>without shedding of blood there is no remission</u>."* **NKJV**. And in **Hebrews 10:11 & 12:** *"And every priest stands ministering daily and offering repeatedly the same sacrifices, which can never take away sins. But this Man, after He had offered one sacrifice for sins forever, sat down at the right hand of God."* **NKJV**.

Chapter 2

Grain Offerings

Now we have the Grain Offering, or the Drink Offering. This sacrifice is a meatless and bloodless offering. This offering was associated with the harvest. It required the best, or the first fruit from the harvest. God always requires our best. Never give anything less than your best to the Lord.

The process of making the Grain Offering or Drink Offering included in the baking of this unleavened bread is olive oil, the best fine grain, frankincense (dried), and salt. **Verses 13, 15 & 16**.

The prepared bread is presented to the priest for him to present to the Lord. **Verse 9**

The purpose of this offering is to <u>offer your best</u>, and the best is what God requires. When this is done, God is well pleased.

I like the old Hymn: <u>Is Your All on the Altar</u>? This hymn was written by Elisha A. Hoffman.

"You have longed for sweet peace and for faith to increase,

And have earnestly, fervently prayed;

But you cannot have rest or be perfectly blessed,

Until all on the altar is laid.

Is your all on the altar of sacrifice laid?

Your heart does the Spirit control?

You can only be blest and have peace and sweet rest,

As you yield Him your body and soul."

Elisha A. Hoffman

An acceptable sacrifice is a full sacrifice, with nothing held back. An acceptable sacrifice is one that is given in humility and with an obedient heart.

Remember, God does not want <u>sacrifice</u>; God wants <u>obedience</u>. Samuel makes this statement to the arrogant King Saul in his disobedience: *"So Samuel said: 'Has the Lord as great delight in burnt offerings and sacrifices, as in obeying the voice of the Lord? Behold, <u>to obey is better than sacrifice</u>, and to heed than the fat of rams.' "* **1 Samuel 15:22 ESV**

Everything about worship, every sacrifice and everything about the Tabernacle, is a photo-type of Jesus Christ who is the Only Begotten Son of God: the Great High Priest, the Lamb of God, the <u>Perfect and Final</u> Sacrifice for the sin of the world. There is no other sacrifice that needs to be made.

Each offering that we go over here in Leviticus is a reminder of what Jesus would do when He came. Jesus was the Lamb of God who was slain for the sin of the world. **Revelation 5:6**: *"And I looked, and behold, in the midst of the throne and of the four living creatures, and in the midst of the elders, stood a Lamb as though it had been slain, having seven horns and seven eyes, which are the seven Spirits of God sent out into all the earth."* **NKJV**.

Let me say this concerning sacrifice for sin: Did you know that God chose to love you, not to hate you? Did you know that the reason God chose to love you was not because of any good thing that you have done? God chose to send His Son Jesus to die for us out of His great love. Paul writes in **Romans 5:8** that while we were still sinning, Jesus died for us.

No one is so good that he does not need forgiveness of sin; and no one is too evil that God would not want to forgive his sin. The blood of Jesus cleanses <u>all sin</u>. God sent Jesus to pay the price of sin. That price was too high for any man to pay, so Jesus came. God is not willing that anyone would die because of sin. His desire is for all to come to repentance. **2 Peter 3:9**.

God doesn't want people to sacrifice for sin; our sacrifice falls short of forgiveness. He has already made the sacrifice for us.

Chapter 3

Peace Offerings

Now we will look at the **Peace Offering**. The Peace Offering is a voluntary sacrifice, and it is actually a sacrifice which includes feasting together and giving thinks with a loving and joyful heart for the blessings of God.

There are three reasons for this love and joy during this Peace Offering: Because of a <u>vow that has been made has been fulfilled</u>, because of <u>a recent blessing</u> from the good hand of God, or <u>out of a mere heart of joy for God</u>.

The Peace Offering is the only sacrifice that the giver and the priests celebrate together. The priestly line was from the tribe of Levi; and they were given the charge of caring for the Tabernacle and assembling and disassembling it. Perhaps we could call the Levites the official "moving company" of the Tabernacle. The Levites prepared the Tabernacle for worship, and they also prepared it for travel.

But in the Peace Offering, those who would share in it were Aaron (the high priest here is Aaron) with his four sons, his ordained assistants. Aaron had four sons, Nadab, Abihu, Eleazar, and Ithamar.

The sacrifice animal for this Peace Offering could be either male or female. **Verse 1**: *"If his offering is <u>a sacrifice of peace offering, if he offers <u>an animal from the herd, male or female, he shall offer it without blemish</u> before the Lord.* **ESV.**

This sacrifice also reminds one of the Last Supper meal in the upper room with Jesus and His disciples; it is recorded in

John 13. Jesus came to overcome the payment of death for sin and to reposition the believer as righteous and acceptable before the Father. It is unbelievable, but it is true. This is the mystery of the Gospel. It is something in which the believer and God rejoice together. The sacrifice of Jesus has presented the believer righteous and acceptable before the Father. **2 Corinthians 5:21**.

There is an unusual statement here: *"All fat is the Lord's."* **Verse 16 ESV**. The intention of this statement is that believers should leave the best of all things for the Lord.

In **Genesis 45:18**, Pharaoh tells Joseph to assure his brothers not to hesitate in bringing the families to Egypt because they will live off the fat of the land, or the best part of Egypt: *"Bring your father and your households and come to me; I will give you the best of the land of Egypt, and you will eat the fat of the land."* **NKJV**.

This promise was not casually given. It was authoritatively given by Pharaoh himself. The believer is to give the best that he has to God and not take any of it for himself.

The aroma from the sacrifice is a sweet smell, or a pleasant aroma, unto the Lord. The fat has been burned. It has been consumed by the Lord. Then there is a command: *"And the priest shall burn them on the altar as a food offering with a pleasing aroma. All fat is the Lord's. It shall be a statute forever throughout your generations, in all your dwelling places, that you eat neither fat nor blood."* **Verses 16 - 17 ESV**

The Peace Offering is the last of the *"voluntary"* sacrifices. Voluntary does not mean *"optional."* It means *of your free will* and out of personal *"obedience"* to God.

In **John 3:16** we read that *"Whosoever believes in Him shall not perish."* This gives no option for eternal life. There is only one way to be given eternal life, and that is for each person to make <u>his own choice</u>, freely and voluntarily, and under no outside pressure.

All sacrifices <u>must</u> be made, but these first three: <u>The Burnt Offering</u>, <u>The Grain or Drink Offering</u>, and <u>The Peace Offering</u> must come from a free choice, and made from of a heart of obedience and love for God.

Chapter 4

Sin Offerings

A Sin Offering is for sins that have been committed. What is sin? Sin is falling short of the glory of God, as we read in **Romans 3:23**. Now, God does not make up laws. Laws are made because of people who have not naturally done what should be done. All mankind has sinned against God; all mankind has trespassed upon His holiness.

What do we know about God? We know that God is love, as we read in **1 John 4:8 – 11**: *"He who does not love does not know God, for <u>God is love</u>. In this the love of God was manifested toward us, that God has sent His only begotten Son into the world, that we might live through Him. <u>In this is love, not that we loved God, but that He loved us and sent His Son to be the propitiation for our sin.</u> Beloved, <u>if God so loved us, we also ought to love one another.</u>"* **NKJV**.

The measure of love is exampled by God. He is perfection, He is pure holiness, and He is love. Not living up to any characteristic of God in the slightest degree is totally falling short of the glory of God. God's measure is perfection.

Sin can be <u>intentional</u> or it could be <u>unintentional</u>; or it could be done <u>ignorantly</u>, meaning that one did not know about a requirement.

All people sin: Good people sin, bad people sin, followers of Christ sin, and respected leaders sin. We all have sinned.

When a sin is committed, there is a price to be paid, and there is an atonement that must be made for that sin.

There are four words that are used in connection with sin:

1. **Sin**: Which is falling short of the glory of God. **Romans 3:23**

2. **Trespass**: Going over the line, or intruding into forbidden territory.

3. **Transgression**: Disobedience, or rebellion, infringement, wrongdoing. Jesus said in the model prayer: Forgive us our transgressions, our debts, and our sins. **Matthew 6:12 – 14.**

4. **Iniquity**: Immorality, unholiness and evil acts. **Jeremiah 17:9 & 10**: *"The heart is deceitful above all things, and desperately wicked; who can know it? I, the Lord, search the heart, I test the mind, even to give every man according to his ways, according to the fruit of his doings." * **NKJV.**

In **Psalm 32:1, 2 & 5**, the Psalmist David mentions each of these: *"Blessed is he whose transgression is forgiven, whose sin is covered. Blessed is the man to whom the Lord does not impute iniquity, and in whose spirit there is no deceit. . . I acknowledge my sin to You, and my iniquity I have not hidden. I said, 'I will confess my transgressions to the Lord.' And You forgave the iniquity of my sin. Selah"* **NKJV.**

When an <u>unintentional</u> sin becomes <u>understood</u>, or is <u>brought to the attention</u> of the one who has sinned, a Sin Offering must be made for that sin. God gives four situations for giving a Sin Offering:

1. The <u>unintentional sin</u> of <u>the anointed priest</u>, bringing guilt. **Verses 1 – 12**. Sacrifice a bull. **Verse 4**

2. The <u>unintentional sin</u> of <u>the whole congregation</u>. **Verses 13 – 21**. Sacrifice a young bull. **Verse 14**

3. The <u>unintentional sin</u> of <u>a leader of the people</u>. **Verses 22 – 26**. Sacrifice a male goat. **Verse 23**

4. The <u>unintentional sin</u> of <u>the average person</u>. **Verses 27 – 35**. Sacrifice a young female goat. **Verse 28**

Each animal offered as a sacrifice must be without blemish, and it must be a perfect animal. Remember, this sacrifice could not wash away, or atone for sins made. The writer of Hebrews writes in **Hebrews 10:1 – 4**: *"For the law, having <u>a</u> <u>shadow of the good things to come, and not the very image of</u> <u>the things</u>, can never with these same sacrifices, which they offer continually year by year, make those who approach perfect. For then would they not have ceased to be offered? For the worshipers, once purified, would have had no more consciousness of sins. But in those sacrifices there is a <u>reminder</u> of sins every year. <u>For it is not possible that the blood of bulls</u> <u>and goats could take away sins.</u>"* **NKJV**.

And in **Hebrews 10:11 – 15**: *"And every priest stands ministering daily and offering repeatedly the same sacrifices, which can never take away sins. But this Man, after He had offered one sacrifice for sins forever, sat down at the right hand of God, from that time waiting till His enemies are made His footstool. For by one offering He has <u>perfected forever</u> those who are being sanctified."* **NKJV**

There is only one way to receive permanent forgiveness of sin, and that is through the blood of Jesus Christ, the Perfect Sacrifice for sins. *"Now where there is remission of these, there is no longer an offering for sin."* **Hebrews 10:18 NKJV**.

Now, all sins are sins against God, whether known or unknown. Because a sin is unknown does not excuse the sin; all sin must be punished whether known or unknown.

When God forgives our sin, He forgives all sin—past, present, and future. God is all knowing, and being all knowing, there is nothing that has ever been done, is being done, or will be done, that He is not fully aware. God knows us completely! While we were still sinners and still in the very act of sinning, Jesus died for us. Isn't that amazing? **Romans 5:8**.

But the children of Israel did not clearly understand about the coming perfect Sacrifice of Jesus. What they must do is to obey, follow, and worship the God and the Father, whom they do know.

These last two sacrifices, The Sin Offering and The Trespass Offering, were mandatory. When one sins, he MUST offer a sacrifice!

In **Verses 1 & 2** here we read: *"And the Lord spoke to Moses, saying, 'Speak to the people of Israel, saying, If anyone sins unintentionally in any of the Lord's commandments about things not to be done, and does any one of them,' "* **ESV**.

Sin is always sin whether you understand it to be sin or not. The Law makes known sin. *"Well then, am I suggesting that the law of God is evil? Of course not! The Law is not sinful, but it was the law that showed me my sin. I would never have known that coveting is wrong if the law had not said, 'Do not covet'."* **Romans 7:7 NLT**.

As the old saying goes: *"ignorance of the law is no excuse."* Let me give you an example: I was taking some courses at Albany State University at night; and one night as I left the classroom and turned onto the main street, I turned right rather than left. There was no traffic, and there was an entrance to a shopping center on the other side of the road; so rather than going completely into the parking lot and turning around, I turned around making a U-turn, but going partially into the shopping center entrance as I turned around. Having completed the U-turn, I continued on my way home. About a minute into by turnabout, I saw some blue lights flashing in my rear-view mirror. It was the police. I pulled over to the side of the road and the officer came to my window and asked: *"Do you know why I stopped you?"* and I said: I guess it was for my turning around back there. The officer said: *"That is what we call a U-turn."* To his response I said: *"I thought that I did that U-turn correctly."* To my ignorance of the law, the officer responded: *"Correctly! There is no such thing as a correct U-turn!"* I thought I was right, but I was 100% wrong. Ignorance of the law is no excuse. When you break the law, you must pay the price.

In **Leviticus 5:17** we read: *"If a person sins, and commits any of these things which are forbidden to be done by the commandments of the Lord, though he does not know it, yet he is <u>guilty and shall bear his iniquity</u>."* **NKJV**.

In **Verses 14 & 28** it is stated: *"when the sin which they have committed <u>becomes known</u>, . . .* and *"or if his sin which he has committed <u>comes to his knowledge</u>, . . ."* **NKJV**. Sacrifice <u>must</u> be made at that time.

In the parable of the <u>*Prodigal Son*</u>, in **Luke 15:17 – 20**, Jesus pointed out about the wayward son: *"But when he came to himself, . . ."* **Verse 17 NKJV."** Or, when his sin became understood by him, he said that he would go back to his father, repent, and ask to be just a servant, in that he had foolishly wasted his inheritance.

When a previously unknown sin becomes known and clear to us, we should ask forgiveness of that sin. Paul writes in **Romans 2:1** that those who think they are righteous are not; they are filthy and guilty: *"Therefore you are <u>inexcusable, O man, whoever you are who judge, for in whatever you judge</u>*

Never think that you are better than another person. You are not; your heart is as desperately wicked as another. What sin is deserving of eternal death? All sin, and <u>that includes your sin</u>. If Jesus is your perfect sacrifice, then your sin has been placed upon Jesus. When one asks forgiveness of his sin, God forgives that sin and lays that sin upon His spotless Son Jesus. Having done that, Jesus becomes the perfect atonement for sin. Now the Father will pour out upon the sinner the righteousness of Jesus in order that the repentant one might be righteous enough for heaven. **2 Corinthians 5:21:** _"For He made Him who knew no sin to be sin for us, that we might become the righteousness of God in Him."_ **NKJV**

Jesus is our righteous atonement for sin.

Chapter 5

Sin and Guilt Offerings

Now we have the Trespass Offering. Have you seen the sign: **NO TRESPASSING! All violators will be shot!** ? What does *no trespassing* mean? It means you are not to cross the property line. That property does not belong to you. It belongs to another person, and if you infringe upon its boundaries, you will be punished.

The trespass is sin, even if it was done accidently, or unknowingly. When the sin becomes understood and known, the one who has sinned must give a Trespass Offering; and this offering is mandatory. **Verse 5**. A trespass is an infringement upon the holiness of God. Some of these infringements are:

- Failure to testify about something that you have witnessed. **Verse 1**.

- If you touch a dead animal, killed in the wild. **Verse 2**.

- If you touch a diseased person. **Verse 3**.

- If you do not fulfill a vow in any way, whether it was made with thought, or made carelessly without thought, you are guilty of sin. **Verse 4**.

The sacrifice for the trespass is to be an <u>unblemished sheep, goat, two turtledoves, or two pigeons</u>. **Verses 6 & 7**. The sacrifice is to be brought to the priest and the priest would offer it, not the people. **Verses 14 – 19**.

The sacrifice procedure is always the same:

- The appropriate sacrifice is brought to the priest and any restitution is made.

- The priest will place his hand upon the sacrifice as an atonement for sin and to pronounce it as an appropriate and holy sacrifice for the sin committed.

- The priest will then kill and prepare the animal or bird for the sacrifice and place it in the appropriate position upon the altar.

Everything about the sacrifice is holy, and when anyone presents a sacrifice to the Lord, the guilty one is to be genuine in his repentance and is to be totally obedient to all the demands of the Lord for forgiveness.

There is no place for sacrilege. Everything about the sacrifice is holy. Be certain that God cannot be fooled. He knows all things, and God hates a prideful heart. When Jesus was on earth, that prideful and arrogant heart was most evident in all the religious leaders. Jesus called them whitewashed tombs that looked nice on the outside but on the inside they were filled with dead men's bones. **Matthew 23:27**: *"Woe to you scribes and Pharisees, hypocrites! For you are like whitewashed tombs which indeed appear beautiful outwardly, but inside are full of dead men's bones and all uncleanness."* **NKJV**.

Always be genuine, be trustworthy, be obedient, and be forgiving of others as God has forgiven you. Don't be a hypocrite. In everything that you do, do all for the glory of God.

Chapter 6

Priestly Duties in Sacrifices

God gives more instructions for the priest in each of the sacrifices. The first instructions are about the <u>Trespass Offerings</u> for lying. God hates lies, false witnesses, proud looks, murderers, deceivers, and workers of evil plans, as we read in **Proverbs 6:16 – 19**. Jesus said that the father of the lie is Satan; he gave birth to it. **John 8:44**: *"You are of your father the devil, and the desires of your father you want to do. He was a murderer from the beginning, and <u>does not stand in the truth, because there is no truth in him</u>. When he speaks a lie, he speaks from his own resources, <u>for he is a liar and the father of it.</u>"* Jesus hates the lie, and Satan hates the truth; and Jesus is The Truth.

The sin here is not only the lie but the reason behind the lying. People seem to think that some lies are okay. Well, there is never a situation where lying is right. What one may call a *little white lie* <u>is a *big black lie* in the eyes of God</u>. God hates a lying tongue!

God is holy, and a holy God cannot look upon unholiness. Lying is unholy!

The next offering covered is <u>The Altar of Burnt Offering</u>, **Verses 8 - 13**. The Altar of Burnt Offering must always be burning, day and night, and ready for sacrifice. **Verses 10 & 13**: *"The fire on the altar shall be kept burning on it; it shall not go out."* **ESV**.

The Altar of Burnt Offering must be carefully maintained, having the ashes from the offerings carried outside the camp to a place that is ceremonially clean. **Verse 11**.

Following the Altar of Burnt Offering comes further instructions for <u>The Grain Offering</u> regarding the ordination of the priest. **Verses 14 – 23**.

This offering was a meatless offering. The instructions for the Grain Offering has to do with the ingredients, the preparation, and the cooking of the bread loaves. **Verses 15 & 17**:

- A handful of fine flour, without yeast, for this is unleavened bread.
- Olive Oil.
- Dried frankincense sprinkled upon the grain.
- Cooked in a pan upon the altar on both sides.
- Offered to the Lord but consumed by the priest

I can relate to the *"sweet aroma"* that is mentioned here. I love the smell of freshly baked bread.

Next comes additional instructions concerning <u>The Sin Offering</u>. **Verses 24 – 30**. It is <u>most holy</u> before the Lord. The place where the priest ate this offering must be holy. Everyone who touches it is made holy. The clothing that was worn while eating the offering must be cleaned in a ceremonially clean place. Only males could participate in this ordination ceremony. Everything about this is holy. **Verses 25, 27, & 29**.

There is a caveat here: If the blood of the sacrifice was used for the sin of the people and sprinkled in the Holy Place, the meat could not be eaten. It must be totally burned. **Verse 30**.

Chapter 7

More Regulations

To trespass is to step over the line into an area that does not belong to you and is not to be entered without permission. To trespass is to disregard the rights of others and infringe upon them. Infringing upon another is a sin. We are to love God first and love others with the same love that we have for ourselves.

The procedure for the priest in preparing and giving the trespass sacrifice is similar to the procedures for the other sacrifices. Everything is holy, or has a divine purpose behind it, and it must be carried out with holiness.

Offered with this <u>Trespass Offering</u> is the bread from the <u>Grain Offering</u>, and all the priests may eat of this offering. **Verses 9 & 10**

The guilt of the Trespass Offering is lying, stealing and doing something that is detrimental to another. The one who is offering this sacrifice must admit his guilt; and there is also included with his admission a restitution payment for whatever he infringed upon the rights of others. **Leviticus 6:1 – 7**.

Next we have the laws concerning the <u>Peace Offering</u>. The Peace Offering was a <u>voluntary offering</u>. It was not a mandatory or required offering; it was offered <u>freely</u>, and out of a heart that was <u>filled with thanksgiving</u>. The Peace Offering included a spotless lamb that was sacrificed, as well as unleavened and leavened bread; it was offered for confession of sin and in thanksgiving for the blessings from the good hand of God. The Peace Offering highlighted the holy attributes of God and celebrated His goodness with the priest and friends.

The regulations for <u>The Peace Offering</u> are covered next, **Verses 11 – 21**. There were three types of Peace offerings:

1. For thanksgiving: Included a lamb and bread. **Verse 12**

2. For the fulfillment of a vow. **Verse 12**

3. As a freewill offering. **Verse 12**

The unleavened bread loaves or cakes were made from blended flour mixed with oil. **Verse 12**. With the unleavened bread, there was also <u>leavened bread</u> as well; leavened bread contained yeast. **Verse 13**.

The priests were to give a <u>heave offering</u>, in which the priest would take one of the loaves, or cakes, into his two hands that were cupped together, and then he would lift the loaf, or heave it to the Lord for His blessing. This specific loaf of bread that was heaved up to the Lord was reserved for the priest to eat **Verse 14**.

Along with the heave offering was the sprinkling of the blood of the spotless lamb on the horns of the Altar of Burnt Offerings. **Verse 14**.

Another requirement was that the lamb and the cakes must be eaten on the day of the sacrifice if the sacrifice was for the repentance of sin. But if the sacrifice was not offered for sin, but specifically for thanksgiving, the uneaten portion of the meat of the sacrifice could be eaten on the next day; however, what was not eaten by the second day must be burned with fire on the third day. **Verse 17**.

The sacrifice was holy. Everything about it was holy, and anyone who might do anything to dishonor it would cause the sacrifice to be void, or of no avail in the forgiveness of sin, and would not be accepted by the holy God. Any such act was blasphemous and sacrilegious to holy God. Any person who might violate these laws must be "cut off" or excommunicated from the people. **Verses 20 & 21**.

This sacrifice reminds the believer of the Last Supper in **John 13**, just before Jesus was offered as The Lamb of God for the sin of the world. Jesus is the Holy High Priest, the Perfect Sacrifice, and all believers benefit from His one-time offering.

The priests benefited from the offerings. They were sustained with portions of each sacrifice. The sacrifice was to the Lord, **Verse 30**; but Aaron and his sons, the priests, had a portion reserved for them, the breast and the right thigh. **Verses 31 – 36**

Note that all of these sacrifices are examples, and representations of how Jesus was the complete and perfect sacrifice for the sin of the world.

In each of these sacrifices, every part of the Tabernacle and the Temple, and every blessing that is experienced by the children of Israel points to Jesus.

The Apostle Paul wrote in **1 Corinthians 10:11:** *"Now all these things happened to them as examples, and they were written for our admonition, upon whom the ends of the ages have come."* **NKJV**.

Paul goes on to admonish the believer to not be as the children of Israel were: They were proud, they were self-righteous, and they thought that their ways were better than God's ways. They thought that they were sufficient for the task, but they fell short. The believer is to listen to the voice of God, obey the command of God, and follow the lead of God.

Make this your desire in life: Don't listen to yourself only and do not depend strictly upon the instruction of others; but listen to God. God will lead in the right way, and His way is the victorious way.

Proverbs 14:12: *"There is a way that seems right to a man, but its end is the way of death"* **NKJV**

Isaiah 30:21: *"Your ears shall hear a word behind you, saying, 'This is the way, walk in it.' Whenever you turn to the right hand or whenever you turn to the left."* **NKJV**

1 Corinthians 10:12 & 13: *"Therefore let him who thinks he stands take heed lest he fall. No temptation has overtaken you except such as is common to man; but God is faithful, who will not allow you to be tempted beyond what you are able, but with the temptation will also make the way of escape, that you may be able to bear it."* **NKJV**.

Romans 15:4: *"For whatever things were written before were written for our learning, that we through the patience and comfort of the Scriptures might have hope."* **NKJV**.

Having given additional instructions concerning the offerings in worship, God turns to His instructions for Aaron, the high priest, and his sons who are his assistants as priests.

Chapter 8

Dedication of the Priests

Did you know that God has a special plan for you, and in that special plan, He neither leaves anything out, nor does He leave anything undone? Yes, God's unique plans for you are personal and perfect. **Jeremiah 29:11**: *"For I know the thoughts that I think toward you, says the Lord, thoughts of peace and not of evil, to give you a future and a hope."* **NKJV**.

As we see here, God has special things for Aaron and his sons. His desire is for them to be pure, clean, and holy unto the Lord and to be an example for others. All things are to be done in order and with excellence.

Having finished His holy requirements and holy procedures for offering sacrifices, God now places His approval upon Aaron the high priest and Aaron's sons (Nadab, Abihu, Eleazar and Ithamar) who were appointed by God to be his assistant priests.

Exodus 6:23: *"Aaron took to himself Elisheba, daughter of Amminadab, sister of Nahshon, as wife; and she bore him Nadab, Abihu, Eleazar, and Ithamar."* **NKJV**.

Exodus 28:1: *"Now take Aaron your brother, and his sons with him, from among the children of Israel, that he may minister to Me as priest, Aaron and Aaron's sons: Nadab, Abihu, Eleazar, and Ithamar."* **NKJV**.

These men are "called of God" to be priests, in the same way as God calls men to be ministers for Him today. Ministers are the "called out ones"; they are called by God to a specific calling or ministry. This calling is paramount in the lives of all ministers of God. Paul makes reference to his calling in **Acts 20:24:** *"But none of these things move me; nor do I count my life dear to myself, <u>so that I may finish my race with joy, and the ministry which I received from the Lord Jesus,</u> to testify to the gospel of the grace of God."* **NKJV**.

Here we see God divinely and publicly ordain His chosen ministers to the holy ministry as His special ministers.

What is included in this ordination service?

- Aaron and his three sons, **Verse 2**
- Anointing oil, **Verse 2**
- One bull for a Sin Offering, **Verse 2**
- Two rams, **Verse 2**
- A basket of unleavened bread, **Verse 2**
- All the people as a witness, **Verse 4**

What was done?

- Aaron and his sons were washed by Moses. **Verse 6**

- All the priestly clothing of the high priest had been washed and symbolically placed upon Aaron. (The tunic, the sash, the robe, the ephod, the belt, the breastplate, with the Urim and Thummin, and the turban with the golden band engraved with the words: HOLINESS TO THE LORD, **Verses 7 – 9**.

- We read that Nadab, Abihu, Eleazar, and Ithamar have placed upon them their appropriate clothing: their priestly coats, sashes, and turbans, **Verse 13**.

Next, Moses anoints the Tabernacle and everything inside the Tabernacle with holy oil. **Verses 10 & 11**.

Now comes the time for the anointing of Aaron and his sons to the ministry to which God has called them. **Verses 12 – 13**. Nadab, Abihu, Eleazar, and Ithamar were clothed and anointed after Aaron. **Verse 13**.

As the sacrifices were carried out, some of the blood of the sacrificed bull was placed on the Altar of Burnt Offerings and the rest of the blood was poured out at the base of the Altar to consecrate it.

Remember what Jesus said about his death? *"No one takes it from Me, but I lay it down of Myself. I have power to lay it down, and I have power to take it again. This command I have received from My Father."* **John 10:18 NKJV**; and **Mark 14:24:** *"And He said to them, 'This is My blood of the new covenant, which is shed for many."* **NKJV**. The Father gave His Son Jesus a command, just as He gave this same command to Aaron and his sons.

After the sacrifice of the bull for a sin offering, Moses then sacrifices the first ram to be sacrificed as a burnt offering. **Verses 18 – 21**

The second ram was sacrificed as a consecration. There is an odd action that was carried out by Moses upon Aaron and his sons. Moses placed some blood from each ram on the right earlobe and upon the big toe of their right foot. What is the significance of this? Perhaps it represented the responsibility of the priests to listen to the voice of God, and then to be swift to go and do what God has made known to them. **Verses 22 – 25**.

In the Great Commission, all believers are to go and make disciples of all nations. **Matthew 28:19 & 20** and **Acts 1:8**. Although God calls special people to be His ministers, Jesus has called all believers to carry the Gospel to the world. All believers are to be quick to hear this call of God and to respond quickly to that call.

Next, Moses anoints the loaves of unleavened bread that were in the basket. He places the loaves on the right thigh of the sacrifice, and then places them in the hands of Aaron, who waves them in the air before the Lord as a holy <u>wave offering.</u>

A portion of the meat is now placed in a pot to be boiled. This portion perhaps was for Aaron and his sons to eat while they were quarantined, or set apart from the rest of the people for seven days and nights as they performed their personal duties for sanctification, and in making atonement inside the Tabernacle. I might point out that this is a guess, and your guess is as good as mine. I do know that the wicked sons of Eli the high priest abused their position as priests to take more of the meat that was not rightfully theirs. We read of the unholy actions of the sons of Eli, Hophni, and Phinehas, who were known go to the person who was sacrificing an animal, and they would confiscate more meat than was rightfully theirs. **1 Samuel 2:12 – 17**.

We have examples of each of the five offerings used in this ordination service of Aaron and his sons and the inauguration of the Tabernacle.   For seven days Aaron and his sons were separated from the people to carry out all that God would have them do as they made atonement for themselves and the people. **Verses 34 & 35**: *"As he has done this day, so the Lord has commanded to do, to make atonement for you. Therefore you shall stay at the door of the tabernacle of meeting day and night for seven days, and keep the charge of the Lord, so that you may not die; for so I have been commanded."* **NKJV**.

Chapter 9

The Priestly Ministry Begins

Numbers have significant meaning in Scripture. Some examples are: The number *six* is considered to be the number of mankind because God created man on the *sixth day of Creation*; the number *seven* is held as the number of God, noting that on the *seventh day of Creation* God rested from His work of Creation and commanded man to rest from his labor (six days he would labor and on the seventh day he must rest from his labor); and the number *eight* is considered as the number of *new beginnings*, for the *eighth day* was the beginning of a new day for mankind to begin his labor. It was his first week after Creation.

The new thing that is seen here is a God-honoring ministry. It is an honor to be chosen to do the work of the Lord, and that work must be done in a God-honoring and God-glorifying manner! Aaron and his three sons now begin this new work. There is no precedent that has been set, only the direct commands of the Lord.

The duties of Aaron, his sons, and soon the Levites, had to do with worship, and in worship there was sacrifice for sin.

What was included in these first sacrifices that Aaron would offer?

First, a perfect *young bull* was selected for Aaron and his sons to offer for a **Sin Offering** for themselves. **Verse 2.** Aaron and his sons must be pure and holy in order to offer sacrifice to the Lord for the people, so they must make sure they are pure and clean before God by making atonement for their personal sins.

God's requirements for the sacrifices of the people are:

- <u>A one-year-old spotless young goat</u> for a **Burnt Offering** for the people. **Verse 3**

- <u>A one-year-old spotless lamb</u> for a **Burnt Offering** for the people. **Verse 3**

- A bull and a ram for a **Peace Offering**. **Verse 4**

- Flour and oil for a **Grain Offering**. **Verse 4**

These sacrifices were the first sacrifices offered in the newly constructed Tabernacle. Aaron offered a **Sin Offering** for himself. **Verses 8 – 11**; a **Burnt Offering** for the people. **Verses 12 – 14**; a **Sin Offering** and **Burnt Offering** for the people. **Verses 15 – 17**.

Following the sin offering, burnt offering and peace offering, Aaron and his sons go into the Tabernacle to attend to their duties there. Following this they come out of the Tabernacle and Aaron raises his hands and pronounces a <u>blessing from the Lord</u> upon the people as the Priest of the Lord. **Verse 22**.

As Aaron completes his duties, suddenly fire from heaven comes down and consumes the offerings that were upon the altar. God is pleased!

This awesome display of God's power causes the people to fall to their knees in reverent worship. **Verse 24**.

Can you imagine how the children of Israel felt, and how awestruck Moses, Aaron and his sons must have felt. But apparently this awesome and majestic event went to the heads of Aaron's two oldest sons, Nadab and Abihu.

They were young, they were untested, they were privileged, and they would prove themselves to be unworthy of the honor given to them by the Lord to be priests of the Lord.

Young people, and young believers, must be careful when they are thrust into areas of responsibility. The Apostle Paul warned Timothy of such temptations. In Paul's letters to young Timothy, he challenges him to fight the good fight. **1 Timothy 1:18 – 20**. Paul instructs Timothy to pray for others and not to have it his aim to seek preeminence. Paul warns Timothy to use the good characteristics of youth but be aware of the pride within it, and that Timothy should give himself to learning and study of Scripture, **1 Timothy 4:12 – 16**. Paul encourages Timothy to be loyal to his calling: **2 Timothy 1:13 & 14**; he instructs him to be strong in the grace and mercy of the Lord: **2 Timothy 2:1**; and to expect difficulties, for they will be preeminent in his life, **2 Timothy 3**. What does this mean to you? It means that you must be diligent in service, have faithful men and women to follow, and be persistent in prayer.

Chapter 10

Nadab and Abihu

This is such a sad chapter. We see two men that have much to offer and have been given much to present to others, but who are completely overcome with pride of position. King Solomon writes that pride comes before a fall in **Proverbs 16:18**. That is what happens here in this chapter.

What was the sin committed here? The sin of Nadab and Abihu was presumptuous sin. What is presumptuous sin? It is sin that is willfully committed and with an attitude that your sin is not that bad.

Charles Spurgeon says this about presumptuous sin: *"All sins are great sins, but yet some sins are greater than others. Every sin has in it the very venom of rebellion, and is full of the essential marrow of traitorous rejection of God. But there be some sins which have in them a greater development of the essential mischief of rebellion, and which wear upon their faces more of the brazen pride which defies the Most High."* **Charles Spurgeon**, from Sermon No. 135 Presumptuous Sins.

The disciples of Jesus struggled with such pride: Their mindset was: Who is the greatest? Their thought was, "I'm better than you are, and I deserve greater opportunity and reward." **Luke 22:24 – 30 & Matthew 18:1 – 5**. Jesus addresses this pride by saying in essence: The least is the most important, or the one who feels he has the least to brag about is the greatest in the Kingdom of God.

Nadab and Abihu felt they had much to brag about, and that they were better than others because they were selected to be priests.

What was wrong with this incense burner or censer filled with incense and fire? They were in The Holy of Holies, where they were not permitted. Only the high priest, and that was Aaron, was permitted there. They were presenting themselves as unstable priests. *"... In this way they <u>disobeyed the Lord <u>by burning before him a different kind of fire</u> than he had commanded."</u>* **Verse 1 NLT**. The fire to be used was to come from the brazen altar, and apparently it did not. *"And the fire on the altar shall be kept burning on it; it shall not be put out. And the priest shall burn wood on it every morning, and lay the burn offering in order on it; and he shall burn on it the fat of the peace offerings. A fire shall always be burning on the altar; it shall never go out."* **NKJV**.

Nadab and Abihu were doing all things wrong. They had the wrong spirit about them; they used the wrong method; they came at the wrong time; they had the wrong motive; and they offered the wrong fire.

The conclusion of their act of sacrilege was: *"So fire went out from the Lord and devoured them, and they died before the Lord."* **Verse 2 NKJV**. It is a fearful thing to fall into the hands of a living God, as we read in **Hebrews 10:31**.

Serving God is not a casual thing; it is a holy thing! *"And Moses said to Aaron, 'This is what the Lord spoke, saying: 'By those who come near Me I must be regarded as holy; I must be glorified.' So Aaron held his peace."* **Verse 3 NKJV**.

Moses calls for the cousins of Nadab and Abihu, Mishael and Elzahpan to carry the bodies of the brothers outside the camp to be buried. It is interesting that God warns the brothers of Nadab and Abihu not to grieve the death of their brothers or they too will die. Why? First of all, they were in the

Tabernacle and they had duties to carry out; and they also had upon them the anointing oil. But this judgment upon Nadab and Abihu had been carried out by the righteous Judge, God Himself; and that judgement itself was righteous and holy. **Verses 6 & 7**.

The sudden and quick deaths of Aaron's two oldest sons leaves him and his other two sons in total shock and speechless. Aaron and his other sons are in the Holy Place where they were to carry out their priestly duties, but now a pause button has been pressed as time continues to click on.

I am certain that Aaron, Eleazar, and Ithamar touched the bodies of Nadab and Abihu, which is against the Tabernacle law, and because of this great tragedy, there would be opportunity for many more laws to be broken. Moses warns them of the danger and that they are in the holy place.

It was God who had brought about the deaths of Nadab and Abihu, and so Moses tells Aaron and his sons that now is not the time <u>for them to mourn</u> the deaths of the two; however, the children of Israel will mourn for them. **Verses 6 & 7**.

Moses warns Aaron and his two sons to focus on the mission at hand and complete it first. **Verses 8 – 15**. Moses instructs Aaron and his sons not to drink wine or strong drink while in the Tabernacle for it would hinder them from thinking clearly. **Verses 8 & 9**.

In **Verses 16 – 18**, Moses asks about the goat offering that was left on the Brazen Altar that had been totally burned up and not eaten by the priest. Aaron, the grief stricken father of the two boys, tells Moses that the offering was presented by Nadab and Abihu, and that God would not approve of him eating in such a time as this. Moses is then satisfied with the answer of Aaron. **Verses 19 & 20**.

This is a sad passage. The priesthood was new. The prescribed method of worship had just been enacted, and perhaps the two sons of Aaron were not taking their priestly duties seriously. I really do not know the exact reason for Nadab and Abihu offering this *"strange fire,"* but I do know the holiness of worship and to whom the glory in worship <u>must be directed</u>. The holiness in worship and the glory to God was infringed upon by the two sons of Aaron, and for that a price is to be paid. Although the brothers may not have clearly understood the severity of their actions, judgment was unleashed upon them by God. God is not mocked: *"Do not be deceived, God is not mocked; for whatever a man sows, that he will also reap."* **Galatians 6:7 NKJV**. We must also understand that to whom much is given, much is required. The boys should have known better. **Luke 12:48:** *"But he who did not know, yet committed things deserving of stripes, shall be beaten with few. For everyone to whom much is given, from him much will be required; and* <u>*to whom much has been committed, of him they will ask the more.*</u>*"* **NKJV**.

Worship should never be just a once a week thing; worship must be an everyday thing. God is worthy of praise and worship all the time!

Why would someone not be in an attitude of worship? I believe that I could say for the same reasons that Nadab and Abihu were judged by God. I believe that some of those reasons that God judged the brothers were:

- They did not listen to God closely.

- They did not obey God in all that He had asked them to do.

- They did not respect His holiness for what it was.

- They did not glorify God alone, but rather they took some of the glory of God for themselves.

Worship is also personal. It is a one-to-One thing; by that I mean that worship is one person worshipping God alone. The worshipper may be in a crowd of people but he must have his eyes focused upon the One God.

Chapter 11

Clean and Unclean Animals

Chapter 11 is a quite mysterious one. Here God declares what creations are clean, and which are unclean. Not only does God declare which creations are clean and unclean, but He distinguishes which things are good to eat and which are not good to eat.

The Bible commentator Elmer Towns says this about this chapter: *"There are four explanations offered for these laws: (1) The distinctions were arbitrary, and known only to God. (2) The unclean are those that were often used in idol worship. (3) The unclean were unclean for hygienic purposes, and they were common carriers of disease. (4) They were symbolic as to the characteristics of sinful man, and the characteristics of the followers of God.* **Elmer Towns**.

However, we do know that Israel was traveling through the wilderness, where there was little to eat, and perhaps God was letting them know the difference between the healthy food and the unhealthy food.

Here is the list that God gives:

<u>Clean animals</u> on the land. **Verses 3 & 4**:

Those that chew the cud and have a divided hoof, such as a cow.

<u>Those excluded</u> from among the above: *Camel, rabbit, pig, coney.*

<u>Clean aquatic beings</u> in the water. **Verse 9**:

Those with fins and scales.

<u>Unclean aquatic beings</u> in the water. **Verses 10 - 12**:

Those without scales.

<u>Unclean birds</u>. **Verses 13 - 18**:

Eagle, vulture, hawk, falcon, raven, ostrich, owl, osprey, gull, stork, heron, bat.

<u>Unclean insects</u>. **Verses 20 & 23**:

Those that walk on all four legs.

<u>Clean insects</u>. **Verse 21**:

Locust, katydid, cricket, grasshopper.

The **New King James Translation** uses the word *"abomination"* to express disgust; while the **English Standard Version** as well as the **New Living Translation** uses the word *"detestable"* for these unclean animals and creatures not to be eaten. As for me, I must say that the overwhelming majority of each of these listed are certainly <u>detestable in my sight</u>. And I believe I can honestly say that the thought has never come to my mind to eat any insect. I must say that, when it comes to insects, swarming creatures, and crawling creatures like lizards and snakes, they are all <u>detestable </u>to me. However, there are many who do eat these things. I'm thinking to myself: "How hungry would I have to be to eat a roach?"

But I guess there were some of the children of Israel who decided to eat some of these things while traveling in the wilderness. Although God met all their needs in the wilderness, at times many felt hungry and thirsty and complained to Moses about food and water. **Exodus 16 & 17**.

Next, God gives laws concerning what a person is to do to clean himself when touching dead things and unclean things, and the <u>things that cause uncleanness</u>. The question is: What is required to be cleansed from that uncleanness? **Verses 24—39**:

I think most people have an innate feeling of uncleanness when coming into contact with the following things. The phrase used in the **New Living Translation** is: *"The following creatures will make you <u>ceremonially unclean</u>."* **Verse 24 NLT**.

<u>*Coming in contact with any unclean thing.*</u> **Verses 24 – 28**.

Touching a dead body. **Verse 24**. The remedy is: Wash your clothing and do not be around anyone for half a day.

<u>*Touching any rodent, lizard, or snake.*</u> **Verses 29 – 38**. The remedy is: clean with water, or if any cooking item is contaminated by any of those mentioned, that item must be broken or discarded because it is of no use anymore. If the water falls on anything in the cleansing process, <u>it is contaminated</u> or polluted One exception is water from a flowing body of water such as a creek; that water <u>is not polluted</u>.

<u>*No creeping thing or crawling thing is to be eaten.*</u> **Verses 42 – 44**. Though some may be considered eatable, they are not holy. *"For I am the Lord who brings you up out of the land of Egypt, to be your God. <u>You shall therefore be holy, for I am holy.</u>"* **Verse 45 NKJV**.

The reason for this whole discourse is to give understanding to what is clean and that which is not clean; to list the things that can be eaten and the things that are not to be eaten. **Verses 46 – 47**: *"This is the law about beast and bird and every living creature that moves through the waters and every creature that swarms on the ground, to make a distinction between the unclean and the clean and between the living creature that may be eaten and the living creature that may not be eaten."* **ESV**

So, how is the believer to understand this chapter, and how does it relate to the New Testament believer's life?

The first thing is the fact that God is holy, and everything that the believer does must be reflective of his life in God, and that he is faithfully following the Only Begotten Son of God, Jesus Christ. *"Therefore, whether you eat or drink, or whatever you do, do all to the glory of God."* **1 Corinthians 10:31 NKJV**.

The next thing that can be applied to the life of a believer is that although some things can be done, it does not mean that they should be done. Do not live your life seeking your will and to do all that you desire to do; live your life seeking to be holy as God is holy. *"You may say, 'I am allowed to do anything.' But I reply, 'Not everything is good for you.' And even though 'I am allowed to do anything,' I must not become a slave to anything."* **1 Corinthians 6:12 NLT**.

The believer lives his life to be pleasing to God, not *"detestable"* to God.

Chapter 12

Purification after Childbirth

One of the miracles of life is to bring into life a child. But though the birth of a child is a wonderful and joyful thing, there is with the joy also great pain in the process. When Adam and Eve sinned, one of the penalties for their sin is recorded in **Genesis 3:16:** *"To the woman He said: 'I will greatly multiply your sorrow and your conception; in pain you shall bring forth children; . . .'"* **NKJV**.

For the mother of the child there is a recovery period of seven days; and if the child born was a male child, the boy child is to be circumcised on the eighth day. After the circumcision of the male child, the mother is to be secluded and resting for thirty-three days. **Verses 1 – 4**.

If the child was a girl, then the mother is to rest for two weeks and then be secluded for sixty-six days. **Verse 5.**

Following the time of rest and recuperation, the mother of the newborn child is to bring the child to the Tabernacle with an offering. The sacrifice is to be a one year old spotless lamb for a burnt offering, and two turtle doves, or two pigeons for a sin offering. **Verse 6**: *"And when the days of her purifying are completed, whether for a son or for a daughter, she shall bring to the priest at the entrance of the tent of meeting a lamb a year old for a burnt offering, and a pigeon or a turtledove for a sin offering, and he shall offer it before the Lord and make atonement for her."* **ESV**

If the mother cannot afford a lamb, she can just bring two turtledoves or two pigeons. *"And if she cannot afford a lamb, then she shall take two turtledoves or two pigeons, one for a burnt offering and the other for a sin offering. And the priest shall make atonement for her, and she shall be clean."* **Verse 8 ESV**.

The duty of the priest is to offer the sacrifices in making atonement for the child and for the dedication of the male child. God always makes a way for repentance to be freely made and available for any who would ask. Repentance is not beyond the capability, or ability, of anyone.

Jesus came to be that full and final sacrifice for sin, and there is nothing left for the believer to bring for the atonement of his sins. Jesus paid the full price. He was the pure and spotless lamb of God, and now is the time for our salvation.

John the Beloved writes in his epistle: **1 John 1:9:** *"If we confess our sins, He is faithful and just to forgive us our sins and to cleanse us from all unrighteousness."* **NKJV**. This verse does not say, "If you can afford" to confess your sins.

The first thing that the believing parent is to do after the time of purification is fulfilled is to take that newborn baby to worship God. The parents are to bring a sacrifice to the Tabernacle and present it to the priest, who will then offer it to the Lord. The sacrifice is to be a one year old lamb as a burnt offering; and to bring two turtledoves, or two pigeons (One for a burnt offering and the other for a sin offering). **Verses 6 – 8**.

After the offerings have been completed, the mother is declared by the priest to be clean. **Verse 8**.

Mary and Joseph apparently were not well off and could not afford a lamb, for we read in **Luke 2** that after the birth of Jesus, Mary and Joseph took Him to the Temple to make this offering, and brought two turtledoves or two young pigeons,

Luke 2:22 – 24: *"Now when the days of her purification according to the law of Moses were completed, they brought Him to Jerusalem to present Him to the Lord. (as it is written in the law of the Lord, 'Every male who opens the womb shall be called holy to the Lord'), and to offer a sacrifice according to what is said in the law of the Lord, 'A pair of turtledoves and two young pigeons.'"* **NKJV**.

How does this relate to the believer? Today we dedicate children to the Lord after they are born, soon after they are born. But dedicating a child to the Lord is the responsibility of believing parents, and it does not end on the day of a child's dedication. This responsibility carries out through the whole life of the child.

This responsibility should be the desire of every believing parent, to bring his children up in the ways of the Lord. Do not leave this responsibility to the church. It is the parents' responsibility! It should be the passion and desire of all believing parents.

Chapter 13

The Lepers

The dreaded disease that is called **Leprosy** in Scripture is called **Hansen's disease** today. There are still areas of the world where it is a problem. There are still leper colonies in India, Brazil, Africa, and Indonesia. However, it is curable if caught early and it is not as rampant as it was in the past. In the past it was one of the most dreaded diseases, as expressed in the Old and New Testament days. Chapters 13 and 14 deal with this dreaded disease and other ones. Leprosy and other such diseases not only affected the body, but they affected their clothing and the houses they lived in and visited, as well as everyone associated with the person who had leprosy.

Leprosy is a skin disease that begins outside the body and eats at it. It was evidenced by how it affected the skin. The diseases that are examined here could be anything from psoriasis to leprosy itself.

The one designated with the responsibility of examining, diagnosing, and treating these diseases was the priest. **Verses 2 & 3:** *"When a person has on the skin of his body a swelling or an eruption or a spot, and it turns into a case of leprous disease on the skin of his body, then he shall be brought to Aaron the priest or to one of his sons the priests, and the priest shall examine the diseased area on the skin of his body. And if the hair in the diseased area has turned white and the disease appears to be deeper than the skin of his body, it is a case of leprous disease. When the priest has examined him, he shall pronounce him unclean.* **ESV.**

Leprosy alienated one from being with friends and family, and it exempted him from public worship. This disease of Leprosy was extremely contagious, and diagnosing the disease must be quick; therefore, everyone was to be on the alert for the *"tell-tell-signs."* What are these signs? <u>A swelling, a rash, or a shiny patch on their body</u>. **Verse 2**. God tells Moses that if the concern is determined to be leprosy, it needs to be diagnosed quickly and treated quickly. Leprosy is <u>a highly contagious skin disease</u>. **Verse 2**.

In the same way, believers are to be alert for "tell-tell-signs" of sin in their lives. What are they?

- <u>Pride.</u> Pride contaminates, **Proverbs 16:18**. Pride develops into a lack of love, and love is replaced by bitterness, wrath, and anger: **Ephesians 4:25 – 32**.

- <u>Greed</u>. **1 John 2:15 – 17**.

- <u>Covetousness</u>. **1 John 2:15 – 17**.

What is the remedy for the pandemic of sin? The remedy is the blood of Jesus Christ. But believers must be quick to recognize sin contaminating his life. The believer must be quick to recognize the lack of love for others, and a decreasing desire to pray and read God's Word. When one recognizes the tell-tell-signs, he must resist the devil, by drawing near to God. This requires the repentant one to be genuinely sorrowful for his evil ways and to stop, cleanse his ways, and to be genuinely sorrowful for his evil ways. **James 4:7 - 19**

The process that the priest took in deciding if the person had this disease or not was: Examine the person, quarantine him for <u>seven days</u>, and then examine again; after seven days the person was to return for a reexamination; and if the priest was still uncertain at that time, if there was some doubt, the priest was to quarantine the person for <u>an additional seven</u>

<u>days</u>. **Verses 4 & 5**: *"When the priest has examined him, he shall pronounce him unclean. But if the spot is white in the skin of his body and appears no deeper than the skin, and the hair in it has not turned white, the priest shall shut up the diseased person for seven days. And the priest shall examine him on the seventh day, and if in his eyes the disease is checked and the disease has not spread in the skin, then the priest shall shut him up for another seven days.* **ESV**.

After <u>14 days</u> the patient is to come back to the priest for him to either declare him clean, or unclean. **Verses 6 – 8**. If the diseased area itched and it was covered with hair, the hair is to be shaved for closer examination by the priest, and if pronounced unclean he was to leave the populated area and to be separated from all people. **Verses 29 – 46**.

Not only were the lepers excommunicated from others, if they were to walk anywhere they were to shout out: *"Unclean! Unclean!* Can you imagine the feeling of hopelessness that they felt?

If the person is declared to genuinely have leprosy, and there are open boils and patches of white skin and flesh, the patient is to be secluded outside the camp, living by himself or herself. Everything that belonged to the leper was to be burnt, washed, scraped, and then destroyed. Just a note here: Dealing with the clothing of a leper, we read the word *"woof"* which a horizontal threading or the cross-stitching in the lining of a garment. *"…If the disease has spread in the garment,* <u>*in the warp or the woof,*</u> *or in the skin, whatever be the use of the skin, the disease is a persistent leprous disease; it is unclean. …"* **Verses 51 & 52 ESV**.

There were many people who suffered from this disease, and there where leper areas or colonies that were established outside many cities. In the days of Jesus and the early Roman Empire, there were areas designated as leper colonies. It is said that Tiberius Caesar contracted leprosy and had sores on his face, and went to live on the island of Capri, perhaps from being diagnosed with leprosy.

We read of four lepers who: *"lived outside of the city"* in **2 Kings 7:3 – 8**. At this time, the Syrian army had surrounded Samaria, the capital city of the Northern Kingdom of Israel, during the reign of Jehoram, and the prophet Elisha. During the night God had caused the mighty Syrian army to run in fear. These four lepers, living outside the city were the first to discover the abandoned Syrian camp; after a while they went to the wall of the city to announce to the starving people of Samaria what had happened.

We read of Jesus coming into contact with many lepers in the time of His ministry. **Matthew 8:1 – 4 & Luke 5:12 – 16**. Jesus was asked by one leper if He was willing to heal a leper; and the quick and short response of Jesus was: *"I am willing; be cleansed."* **Luke 17:11 – 19**. Just that quick they were healed and told to go to the priest for him to examine them and pronounce them clean. They were among those who stood afar off and cried out, *"unclean, unclean!"* These men were bad news and lived among the unclean, but now they were among those who spread the Good News of Jesus to make them clean!

The lepers was easily seen and heard. They were distinguished by: <u>Unkept hair, torn clothing, covered mouth, and shouting out: Unclean! Unclean</u>!

Verses 45 & 46: *"The leprous person who has the disease shall wear torn clothes and let the hair of his head hang loose, and he shall cover his upper lip and cry out, 'Unclean, unclean.' He shall remain unclean as long as he has the disease. He is unclean. He shall live alone. His dwelling shall be outside the camp."* **Verses 45 & 46 ESV**.

It was as though the leper were saying: I am unworthy to be around you! But that was not what Jesus thought. Jesus told those whom He healed of these diseases: Go show yourself to the priest. **Matthew 8:4:** *"And Jesus said to him, 'See that you tell no one; but go your way, <u>show yourself to the priest,</u> and offer the gift that Moses commanded, as a testimony to them."* **NKJV**.

Jesus did not exclude the lepers from his ministry. He encouraged them to come to Him, and He commanded His disciples to reach out to them and heal them as well. Leprosy excluded people, but Jesus included them.

The leper was in need of:

- <u>The High Priest,</u> and that was Jesus our great High Priest.

- <u>Healing at the hand</u> of The Great Physician, and that Is Jesus.

- <u>Someone to worship and praise,</u> and Jesus is the only One worthy of genuine worship and praise.

The mission of Jesus was to supply the remedy for sin. There is only one remedy, and that remedy is the blood of Jesus. Jesus is the only answer to our sin problem and the source of our problem is the disease of sin. Sin entered into our life through one man, Adam, and it brought eternal death. But there was also One Man, Jesus Christ, who has brought eternal life, **Romans 5:12 – 21**.

The application of the remedy is quick, permanent, and sure. The work was done by Him alone, and that offering was His offering, His final sacrifice, **Hebrews 10:11 – 18**. The blood offering of Jesus gives justification for God The Father to pour out the righteousness of Jesus upon all who would believe in His Son, Jesus Christ. It cleanses one of this pandemic of sin. **2 Corinthians 5:21.**

I love the Gospel Song written by J. Edwin Orr, "<u>Search Me O God</u>." It was taken from **Psalm 139**:

Search Me O God

Search me, O God, and know my heart today;

Try me, O Savior, know my thoughts, I pray.

See if there be some wicked way in me;

Cleanse me from every sin and set me free.

J. Edwin Orr

The plea of David in Psalm 139 was for God to search him, to examine him, and to see if there was any wicked way in him, and then to reveal that evil way to him. God does not have to examine us. He already knows us thoroughly. What David was saying was for God to reveal to him the evil that was causing his sinfulness.

This is what Jesus, our Great High Priest, has done; He knows us completely, He has always known us completely, and even though He knows us completely, He still died for us! **Romans 5:8**. Everyone needs cleansing of sin, and Jesus has the cleansing power.

Chapter 14

Cleansing of Lepers

Leprosy is extremely contagious, and in **Chapters 13 and 14** there is great detail given in cleansing a leper, his house, his clothing, and everything that he may have touched. The cleansing process requires much of the priest and strict obedience by the healed leper and his family. If the leprous person has been healed of the disease, he must be bought to the priest; and the priest would then go outside of the camp where the people are housed and examine the leper. **Verse 3**.

I find it a comfort to know for certain that Jesus left His perfect home in heaven to come to this unclean earth, filled with unclean sinners, to wash the believing sinner in His precious cleansing blood, making the sinner pure and clean, and then to pronounce the believing sinner clean and holy and able to boldly stand before God The Father. It is a joy to know that because of the cleansing blood of Jesus, God The Father is justified in allowing that believing sinner to enter the New Heaven and the New Earth and to be free to worship Him in the New Jerusalem. Jesus came to us to live among us and to cleanse us from the eternal death of sin; and if we would believe on Him, God The Father would pronounce the believing one clean.

Jesus came to where we are to make us acceptable to go where we could not go on our own. Jesus lived in His holy city, inhabited with His holy angels. Mankind cannot go there; he must be taken there by the pronouncement of God. What is that pronouncement? *"... 'Well done, good and faithful servant;*

you were faithful over a few things, I will make you ruler over many things. <u>Enter into the joy of your Lord</u>.'" **Matthew 25:21 NKJV**

We read in **Matthew 9:12 & 13**, *". . . 'Those who are well have no need of a physician, but those who are sick. . . . 'I desire mercy and not sacrifice.' For I did not come to call the righteous, but sinners, to repentance."* **NKJV**.

The Gospel songwriter Squire Parsons wrote the song, "<u>He Came to Me</u>." The lyrics of this song present the relationship of the leper to spiritually diseased mankind, who are living outside the City of God and cannot go there on their own. What they need is a Great High Priest to heal them and pronounce them clean; and Jesus is that Great High Priest.

Consider and think about this first verse and chorus of "<u>He Came to Me</u>":

He Came to Me

The gulf that separated me from Christ, my Lord,

It was so vast the crossing I could never ford;

From where I was to His domain, it seemed so far,

I cried, "Dear Lord, I cannot come to where you are!"

He came to me, O, He came to me.

When I could not come to where he was, He came to me.

That's why He died on Calvary,

When I could not come to where He was,

He came to Me.

Squire Parsons

The next verses deal with how the children of Israel are to respond to an outbreak of leprosy as they possess that new land. **Verses 33 – 57**.

When the discovery of leprosy is found in a household, the owner of the house is to quickly go to the priest, and then the priest will come to examine the situation and home. If leprosy is confirmed by the priest, the whole house must be emptied, and everything must be washed by the owner of the house. When the cleansing process has been completed and a quarantine period of seven days has elapsed, the owner of the house is to return to the priest and then the priest will come back and re-examine the disease, the house, and the situation.

If the situation is found to be still present, and the whole house is contaminated with an infectious mildew, the contaminated house must then be completely torn down and the material of the building disposed outside the city. Also, if anyone has visited or spent the night in the house, they must wash all their clothing to rid them of the disease. **Verses 43 – 47**.

That was the worse-case scenario. The hope of the household is that when the priest returns for his re-examination of the person and the house, that he will not see any advancement of the disease. **Verses 48**.

If the house has been pronounced *"Clean"* by the priest, then the owner of the house is to offer a sacrifice. The person is to bring two birds: One bird is sacrificed, and the other bird is dipped into the blood of the sacrificed bird. The blood of the sacrificed bird is then sprinkled about the house with a hyssop branch that has been dipped into the blood; this procedure is done seven times, and then the living bird is released into a field outside of town. Why is the house sprinkled seven times? Perhaps it is because seven is the number of completion, the number of perfection, and it is also the number of God.

This act is an act of atonement, or appeasement to God. God tells Moses that this process is to be used with any infectious mildew or contagious disease that may come upon the people as they enter the new land of Canaan. The instructions must be followed to the smallest degree.

Remember, God is perfect. He is holy, spotless, and clean; no unclean thing can come before God.

Isaiah writes in **Isaiah 64:6**: *"But we are <u>all like an unclean thing</u>, and <u>all our righteousnesses are like filthy rags</u>; we all fade as a leaf, and our iniquities, like the wind, have taken us away."* **NKJV**.

In the book of Psalms we read: *"There is none righteous, no not one,"* **Psalm 14:3**. God is the only One who can justify the ungodly, **Romans 4:5**; and the only remedy for sin is Jesus. He is the only acceptable sacrifice for the atonement of sin, **Hebrews 10:12 – 14:** *"But this Man, after He had offered one sacrifice for sins forever, sat down at the right hand of God, from that time waiting till His enemies are made His footstool. For by one offering He has perfected forever those who are being sanctified."* **NKJV**.

Know this: God hates sin with a perfect hatred, and He loves the believer with perfect love. David asked for God to search him for impurities, and the believer should ask God to search him for imperfections in his life. When David asked God to investigate his life, it was not for God to "discover" anything that David was hiding from God, but that God would make known to David any unknown wickedness in his life of which he was unaware.   David writes in **Psalms 139:23 & 24**, *"Search me, O God, and know my heart; try me, and know my anxieties; and see if there is any wicked way in me, and lead me in the way everlasting."* **NKJV**.

Many times the mind of believers is not in sync with the holy mind of Christ, because their mind has been infected with the highly contagious philosophy of the world. When our minds are infected with the world, then we cannot be "ceremonially clean" before God and cannot worship Him in spirit and in truth.

Jesus told the woman at the well: *"God is Spirit, and those who worship Him must worship in spirit and truth."* **John 4:24 NKJV**.

Seek to be clean before God, not before men. Have the mind of Christ Jesus, not the mind of the world. *"Let this mind be in you which was also in Christ Jesus,"* **Philippians 2:5 NKJV**. What was the mind of Christ? He sought to do the complete will of The Father; He desired to bring others to do the will of The Father; and He focused His eyes upon the will of The Father. He was not deterred in any way from doing the will of The Father; and He was not influenced by the thoughts of any others. **Philippians 2:1 – 18**. That is the mind of Christ.

Chapter 15

Cleansing the Body

No one really wants to be unclean. My mom said many times: *"You may be poor and can do nothing about it; but everyone can be clean. You can do something about that."* **Kathleen Taylor Thomas**.

In this chapter God deals with various chronic bodily discharges. They can be either natural or unnatural; and they can be the evidence of various highly contagious diseases. The first concern is with the natural uncleanness coming from genital contamination.

Why is this chapter included in Leviticus? It is because God is concerned with the wellbeing and cleanliness of His children. God wants His children to be known for their cleanliness. We read in Scripture*: Be holy* (pure and clean) *for I am holy* (pure and clean). **Leviticus 19:1; 1 Peter 1:16**.

Another reason for this topic being addressed here is that this cleanness actually separated the children of Israel from the other idol worshippers. Fertility rituals were a common thing in various religions; temple prostitutes were housed and used as part of various fertility rituals in pagan worship.

God desires for His people to be clean in body, mind, and spirit as they come to worship Him. Therefore, God gives instructions concerning how to prepare for worship. The followers of Jesus are to worship God with a clean body, a clean mind, and a clean heart.

The process of ritual cleansing has been covered in the preceding chapters which God gave to Moses, and he made them known to the children of Israel.

- **Chapter 11**: Diet
- **Chapter 12**: Childbirth
- **Chapters 13 & 14**: Skin diseases
- **Chapter 15**: Bodily discharges.

There is one thing that sticks out in my mind, and that is the importance of the washing of the hands.

Do you remember your mother saying: *"Wash your hands first!"*? My wife Bobbie is always using the old adage: *"Cleanliness is next to godliness!"* I need to stress that this is not a Bible passage, but it is a good practice. This adage gained popularity from being part of a sermon that **John Wesley** preached in 1778. I would say that he most likely heard that preached from his mother as he grew up.

In **Chapter 15** God deals with both the uncleanness that comes from <u>natural uncleanness</u>, and <u>unnatural uncleanness</u> which comes from sinful acts. This reminds one of the natural presence of sin. Uncleanness comes from falling short of the glory of God. We can relate that to the common condition of all people: *"For all have sinned and fall short of the glory of God."* **Romans 3:23 NKJV**.

The natural uncleanness is of great importance for all believers to be aware; and they must be sure that they "cleanse themselves" of their natural uncleanness when going to worship God. Separate the natural things from the spiritual. Don't mix sacred things with common things. Be careful, be clean, and be holy before God.

Again, this uncleanness here is not because of wrong deeds. It is because of the natural uncleanness of natural man; this uncleanness comes as part of living life. The unnatural uncleanness is covered in the last section of **Chapter 15**.

When a person has come into contact with a person with either a chronic natural or an unnatural discharge, he is to wash himself thoroughly, and with thought.

Next, God deals with chronic unnatural flows or discharges from the genitals. Such discharges are highly contagious, and careful concern must be taken. If someone comes into contact with a person with a chronic and unnatural discharge, he is unclean, and he must wash himself and anything that may have been around that person.

A sacrifice is to be given by any woman who has had an unnatural flow of blood. After she has been free of the discharge for seven days, she is to bring two turtledoves or two pigeons to the priest for him to offer as both a sin offering and a burnt offering for her atonement. **Verses 28 – 30**.

In **Verse 31** the reason is revealed: *"Thus you shall keep the people of Israel separate from their uncleanness, lest they die in their uncleanness by defiling my tabernacle that is in their midst."* **ESV**

We read in **Mark 5:25 – 34** where Jesus came into contact with a woman who had a <u>flow of blood</u> for 12 years and had spent all that she had in search of a cure. She had suffered from many malpractices of various physicians, but all to no avail.   This woman was totally hopeless and greatly devastated by that disease.

Now she meets the Great Physician who heals all diseases with the words from His mouth. The conclusion of the meeting was a healing and a reason for worship. She had not been clean for over 12 years and, therefore, was unable to worship during that period; but now she was clean! The cleansing came from the mouth of Jesus; and she had been washed with the pure and Living Water from Him. Jesus said to her: *"… Daughter, your faith has made you well. Go in peace, and be healed of your affliction."* **Mark 5:34 NKJV**.

The hymn writer Phoebe Palmer wrote the hymn, *"The Cleansing Wave."* The lyrics are:

The Cleansing Wave

"Oh, now I see the crimson wave!

The fountain deep and wide;

Jesus, my Lord, mighty to save,

Points to His wounded side.

The cleansing stream I see, I see!

I plunge, and, oh, it cleanses me!

Oh, praise the Lord, it cleanses me!

It cleanses me, yes, cleanses me."

Phoebe Palmer

Yes, there is power in the very name of Jesus! Jesus came to seek, save, and to cleanse that which was lost. **Luke 19:10**.

Chapter 16

The Day of Atonement

What does atonement mean? Atonement is an appeasement for sin. Sin is falling short of the glory of God, and sin invaded the world by the disobedience of Adam and Eve to the command of God: *"And the Lord God commanded the man saying, 'Of every tree of the garden you may eat; <u>but of the tree of the knowledge of good and evil you shall not eat, for in the day that you eat of it you shall surely die.'"</u>* **Genesis 2:16 & 17 NKJV**.

Sin was given birth through Adam and Eve believing the lie of Satan, the father of the lie: *". . . Then the serpent said to the woman, 'You will not surely die. For God knows that in the day you eat of it your eyes will be opened, and you will be like God, knowing good and evil.' . . ."* **Genesis 3:1 – 6 NKJV**.

In **Romans 5: 12 – 21**, the Apostle Paul mentions this death sentence for sin and that there is only one remedy for the death sentence for sins committed: *"Therefore, just as through one man sin entered the world, and death through sin, and thus death spread to all men, because all sinned— . . . . (For if by the one man's offense death reigned through the one, much more those who receive abundance of grace and of the gift of righteousness will reign in life through the One, Jesus Christ.) . . . For as by one man's disobedience many were made sinners, so also by one Man's obedience many will be made righteous. Moreover the law entered that the offense might abound. <u>But where sin abounded, grace abounded much more, so that as sin reigned in death, even so grace might reign through</u>*

righteousness to eternal life through Jesus Christ our Lord." **NKJV**.

One way of expressing this pure atonement made by Jesus Christ is: *God's <u>desire to forgive</u> us of all sin, is greater than our <u>ability to sin</u>.* Peter writes in **2 Peter 3:9**: *"The Lord is not slack concerning His promise, as some count slackness, but is longsuffering toward us, <u>not willing that any should perish but that all should come to repentance.</u>"* **NKJV**.

This is not to say that a believer is free to sin as much as he desires, knowing that God will forgive; that is a lie. The Apostle Paul addresses this very thought process in **Romans 6:1 – 14**: *"What shall we say then? <u>Shall we continue in sin that grace may abound? Certainly not!</u> How shall we who died to sin live any longer in it. . . . For sin shall not have dominion over you, for you are not under law but under grace."* **NKJV**

If someone has such a mindset about life in Christ Jesus, then there is a real reason for him to question <u>the genuineness</u> of his salvation. Such a person is one <u>who just **says** that he is</u> part of the family of God; this person is not to be followed. The believer is to be like Christ Jesus and have the mind of Christ Jesus. John the Beloved writes in **1 John 2:19**: *"<u>They went out from us, but they were not of us;</u> . . . but they went out that <u>they might be made manifest,</u> that <u>none of them were of us.</u>"* **NKJV**. They say they are believers, but they are not.

And in **Romans 3:23 – 26**, *". . . being justified freely by His grace through the redemption that is in Christ Jesus, whom God set forth as a propitiation* (atonement) *by His blood, through faith, to demonstrate His righteousness, because in His forbearance <u>God had passed over the sins</u> that were previously committed, <u>to demonstrate at the present time His righteousness,</u> that <u>He might be just and the justifier of the of the one who has faith in Jesus.</u>"* **NKJV**.

And in **Romans 5:6 – 11** Paul writes, *"For when we were still without strength, in due time Christ died for the ungodly. . . . But God demonstrates His own love toward us, in that while we were still sinners, Christ died for us. . . . we have now received the reconciliation."* **NKJV**.

Atonement gives holy reason for the wrath of God to be justly and righteously satisfied; and the act of atonement by Jesus Christ is the ransom price for sin. The atonement that was made by our Great High Priest, Jesus Christ, purified the believer completely. There is nothing left undone and nothing new that must be added to His atonement; it was a "one time" thing.

Atonement makes a person a <u>new </u>person, a <u>new</u> creation, and a <u>holy</u> child of God. What was that atonement? It was the blood of Jesus Christ that atones for sin. **1 John 2:2**: *"And He Himself is the propitiation* (atonement) *for our sins, and not for ours only but also for the whole world."* **NKJV**.

God tells Moses to make sure that Aaron is careful to carry out his duties as high priest exactly as God has instructed him and not to stray from His commands in the slightest manner.

That is what Aaron's sons, Nadab and Abihu, had done. They offered a different kind of fire to light the Altar of Incense. Most likely they thought there was no real need to go back to the Altar to get the fire; but they were wrong, DEAD WRONG. God was offended by their lack of adherence to His Holy demands.

Never feel that your way of worship, or your understanding of a life in Christ Jesus, is just as sufficient as what Jesus has commanded and exampled before us. Your way is the wrong way; your understanding is always to be in question if it cannot be supported by Scripture. And in the same way, the teachings of others are not to be followed, or believed, if they are not supported by clear Scripture. There is only one way and that is the way of Christ Jesus.

Dr. David Jeremiah has written: *"The teachings of Jesus were true:*

- *He is the truth, so we can know Him,*
- *He fulfills the truth, so we can trust Him,*
- *He tells the truth, so we obey Him,*
- *He models the truth, so we can emulate Him,*
- *He predicts the truth, so we can expect Him,*
- *He comforts us with the truth so we can love Him."*

- David Jeremiah

It is always right to do right, to make the right decisions, regardless the repercussions. It is always wrong to make wrong decisions in fear of the repercussions that making a right decision might create.   Jesus is our example, and He came to do the will of His Father, while clearly knowing the repercussions.

Never do things <u>your way</u>; do all things <u>God's way</u>. God's way is the way of truth. Any other way is a lie; and those ways lead to death and eternal death, while God's way leads to life and eternal life.

The instructions that God is giving are for the <u>Day of Atonement</u>. The Day of Atonement comes once a year. This day is also called <u>Yom Kippur</u>, and it is celebrated on the 10th day of the 7th month of the Jewish calendar.

The purpose for the high priest entering into the Holy of Holies is to make atonement by dipping his finger into the blood taken from the Sin Sacrifices, and sprinkling it seven times upon the Ark of the Covenant for the sins of the nation.

However, before the high priest can safely enter the Holy of Holies, he must wash and clean himself, and then <u>he must offer a sacrifice for "himself" to make sure that he is clean</u>.

God cannot use an unclean person in His service. *"But in this way Aaron shall come into the Holy Place: with <u>a bull</u> from the herd for a sin offering <u>and a ram</u> for a burnt offering."* **Verse 3 ESV**.

After Aaron has washed himself and sacrificed for himself, he was then to take <u>two goats</u> from the congregation. <u>One is to be offered as a sacrifice</u> for the sins of the congregation, and <u>the other let go</u>.

To determine which goat is to be sacrificed, Aaron will take from the pocket in the breastplate of his priestly robe the **Urim and Thummin** *(Leviticus 8:8.)* and cast lots to determine which goat is to be sacrificed and which will have the blood of the sacrificed goat sprinkled on its head; and then that goat is let go into the wilderness outside the camp. *"Then Aaron shall cast lots for the two goats: one lot for the Lord, and the other lot for the scapegoat."* **Verse 8 NKJV**.

This freed goat is called the <u>scapegoat</u>. **Verses 20—22:** *"And when he has made an end of atoning for the Holy Place and the tent of meeting and the altar, he shall present the live goat. And <u>Aaron shall lay both his hands on the head of the live goat, and confess over it all the iniquities of the people of Israel, and all their transgressions, all their sins</u>. And he shall put them <u>on the head of the goat and send it away into the wilderness</u> by the hand of a man who is in readiness. The goat shall bear all their iniquities on itself to a remote area, and <u>he shall let the goat go free</u> in the wilderness."* **ESV**. With the offering of the goat is a bull sacrificed as sin offering as well. **Verse 11**.

After all this, the blood of the bull is sprinkled with the finger of the high priest upon the mercy seat of the Ark of the Covenant seven times. **Verse 14**

The blood of the chosen goat is then sprinkled upon the mercy seat housed behind the veil as was the blood of the bull. **Verses 14 – 16**: *"And he shall take some of the blood of the bull and sprinkle it with his finger on the front of the mercy seat on the east side, and in front of the mercy seat he shall sprinkle some of the blood with his finger seven times. "Then he shall kill the goat of the sin offering that is for the people and bring its blood inside the veil and do with its blood as he did with the blood of the bull, sprinkling it over the mercy seat and in front of the mercy seat. Thus he shall make atonement for the Holy Place, because of the uncleannesses of the people of Israel and because of their transgressions, all their sins. . . ."* **ESV**.

This procedure is to be observed from generation to generation forever. **Verse 34**: *"And this shall be a statute forever for you, that atonement may be made for the people of Israel once in the year because of all their sins." And Aaron did as the Lord commanded Moses.* **ESV**

We can see the final cleansing and atonement that Jesus, our Great High Priest, made as He exampled it to His disciples at the Last Supper, recorded in **John 13**. Jesus washed His disciples' feet, and He fed them with the symbol of His blood and His broken and sacrificed body.

Serve God with a clean heart, a clean mind, and a pure purpose, free of any personal glory.

Chapter 17

The Place of Sacrifice

What is seen here in Chapter 17 is the significance of the blood. **Verse 14**: *"For the life of every creature is its blood: its blood is its life."* **ESV**

What does that say to us? It says that the beginning of life is the presence of blood. When does that occur? Blood is the fluid that carries all that is needed in sustaining life, and making you into who you are. We know from medical science that when the fertilized egg attaches itself to the wall of the uterus, bleeding can occur. Life is in the blood.

The caution that is made in this chapter is that all sacrifices must be made at the Altar of Burnt Offering. Any other sacrifice is an idol worship. *"And the priest shall throw the blood on the altar of the Lord at the entrance of the tent of meeting and burn the fat for a pleasing aroma to the Lord. So they shall no more sacrifice their sacrifices to goat demons, after whom they whore. This shall be a statute forever for them throughout their generations."* **Verses 6 & 7 ESV**

Israel will have a huge problem with idol worship. God calls this **spiritual adultery**: "Playing the harlot" and "whoring after other gods." It is described in **Judges 2:17:** *"Yet they would not listen to their judges, but they played the harlot with other gods, and bowed down to them. They turned quickly from the way in which their fathers walked, in obeying the commandments of the Lord; they did not do so."* **NKJV**.

These laws of God applied to everyone in the camp. God expects obedience. He expects to be the focus of all worship, and worship must be from the heart of the worshiper. It must be genuine.

Blood is the only thing that can be used in the atonement for sins. The writer of Hebrews writes in **Hebrews 9:22**: *"And according to the law almost all things are purified with blood, and <u>without shedding of blood there is no remission</u>."* **NKJV**.

The blood of Jesus is the precious cleansing power of all sin. *"So Christ was offered once to bear the sins of many. To those who eagerly wait for Him He will appear a second time, apart from sin, for salvation"* **Hebrews 9:28 NKJV**.

This message from God to Moses was to be given to Aaron and his sons, Eleazar and Ithamar, and is of great importance. Remember, Aaron's two older sons, Nadab and Abihu, had been killed by the Lord because of using *"strange fire,"* or a different source of fire than the Lord had commanded. **Leviticus 10**.

Careful attention <u>must</u> be taken as the duties of the priesthood are carried out. There is no way that is "just-as-good" as the way that God commanded. There is no substitute. It is God's way or no way at all. That is still true today. Never fall to any "new doctrine" that is propagated in the church. There is no "new gospel." There is only "The Gospel" of Jesus Christ. It remains the same through all generations. The Apostle Paul warns Timothy of the danger of false doctrines in **1 Timothy 4:1 – 5**.

Be confident that God still speaks today through His Holy Spirit, guiding men in the way that He would have them to go! He has never stopped speaking. Although we may not listen, God is speaking. However, God never says anything that adds to what is already written in Scripture; and He never guides any believer in any way that is in conflict with what He has already said in Scripture.

There is a caution that is given about eating and drinking blood as well. Because blood is the sustainer of life, people are to respect life. Never kill an animal just for the <u>sport</u> of killing. If an animal is killed and not used for the sustaining of life, that animal is to be buried, covered with soil. *"No person among you shall eat blood, neither shall any stranger who sojourns among you eat blood. "Any one also of the people of Israel, or of the strangers who sojourn among them, who takes in hunting any beast or bird that may be eaten shall pour out its blood and cover it with earth. For the life of every creature is its blood: its blood is its life. . . "* **Verses 13 & 14 ESV**

Remember, God gave to Adam the responsibility of caring for the land and animal life as well. **Genesis 2:15:** *"Then the Lord God took the man and put him in the garden of Eden <u>to tend and keep it</u>."* **NKJV**.

Never have a casual view of the life of any animals. Animals have been given to mankind as a blessing from God. Always respect that blessing from God's hand.

Chapter 18

Pure Sexual Relations

After expressing the sin of not being faithful to God with the people, God now speaks with Moses about one of the most selfish and grievous sins; and this is sexual sins. It is the sin of not being faithful to others. Associated with these sexual sins is idol worship.

Immorality has always been rampant on this earth. Why is that so? Immorality pollutes the blessing of God. God is holy, and He is to be worshiped in holiness and truth. **John 4:24:** *"God is Spirit, and those who worship Him must worship in spirit and truth."* **NKJV**. In **Leviticus 19:1** God says: *"And the Lord spoke to Moses, saying, 'Speak to all the congregation of the children of Israel, and say to them: You shall be holy, for I the Lord your God am holy.' "* **NKJV**.

God is holy and pure, and those who worship God must live in a holy and pure lifestyle. God made sex to be holy and pure; it was for a man and his wife alone. During God's act of Creation, He said that it was not good that man should be alone, and so He made for Adam, Eve. God made her because there was no suitable partner for man. *"And the Lord God said, 'It is not good that man should be alone; I will make him a helper comparable to him.' "* **Genesis 2:18 NKJV**.

Having made woman, God said: *"Therefore a man shall leave his father and mother and be joined to his wife, and they shall become one flesh. And they were both naked, the man and his wife, and were not ashamed."* **Genesis 2:24 & 25 NKJV**.

In the book of Hebrews we read: *"Marriage is honorable among all, and the bed undefiled; but fornicators and adulterers God will judge. Let your conduct be without covetousness; be content with such things as you have. . . ."* **Hebrews 13:4 & 5 NKJV**.

Immorality is always a part of riots, rebellions, wars and insurrection of all types. Immorality is selfishness, covetousness, lustfulness, greed, and pride. Immorality bleeds and rapidly grows with all types of vile emotions.

The Apostle Paul writes of the spiraling increase of immorality in **Romans 1:24 – 28**: *"So God let them go ahead and do whatever shameful things their hearts desired. As a result they did vile and degrading things with each other's bodies. Instead of believing what they knew was the truth about God, they deliberately chose to believe lies. So they worshiped the things God made but not the Creator himself, who is to be praised forever. Amen. That is why God abandoned them to their shameful desires. Even the women turned against the natural way to have sex and instead indulged in sex with each other. And the men, instead of having normal sexual relations with women, burned with lust for each other. Men did shameful things with other men and as a result suffered within themselves the penalty they so richly deserved. When they refused to acknowledge God he abandoned them to their evil minds and let them do things that should never be done."* **NLT**.

Satan polluted God's pure blessing for man with a selfishness of self-pride, a covetousness for what is not his, and a lust for personal satisfaction over the wellbeing of others. God is pure, and all that a believer does must be pure, clean, and holy before God.

From these moral laws are formed the moral laws of most nations. God tells Moses not to use the lustful ordinances of pagan nations as a pattern for living, but to pattern themselves to be a holy nation. God's way is the holy way. *"Therefore, to you who believe, He is precious; but to those who are disobedient, 'The stone which the builders rejected has become the chief cornerstone,' and 'A stone of stumbling and a rock of offense.' They stumble, being disobedient to the word, to which they also were appointed. But you are a chosen nation, His own special people, that you may proclaim the praises of Him who called you out of darkness into His marvelous light; who once were not a people but are now the people of God, who had not obtained mercy but now have obtained mercy."* **I Peter 2: 7 – 10 NKJV**.

The Children of Israel, and today the followers of Christ Jesus, are to be a beacon of light into a world of darkness.

Immorality was often a part of pagan worship. God warns Moses to flee any such association with the worship of Almighty God.

The Canaanite people were idol worshippers: They sacrificed their children in worship; and sexual freedom was actually encouraged.

God gives his laws of sexual purity, *"You shall observe My judgments and keep My ordinances, to walk in them: I the Lord your God. You shall therefore keep My statutes and My judgments, which if a man does, he shall live by them: I am the Lord."* **Verses 4 & 5 NKJV**.

These are God's statutes of morality. God declares that His people who are called by His name are not to have sexual relations with:

- <u>Any close relative</u>: Parent, sister, half-sister, granddaughter, aunt, uncle, daughter-in-law. **Verses 6 – 18**

- <u>Any woman during her menstrual cycle</u>. **Verse 19**

- <u>Any neighbor's wife</u>. **Verse 20**

- You shall not sacrifice your children. **Verse 21**

- You shall not be involved in homosexual acts. **Verse 22**

- You shall not have sex with animals. **Verse 23**

These things are detestable, and sickening to even read, but we must know that they are sins against people and against God, for God is holy. Believers are not to even be associated with anyone who is involved in any of these things. It is the believer's duty to rescue them.

God describes the detestable immorality of the Canaanite people whose land God has given Israel: *"(for the people of the land, who were before you, did all of these abominations, so that the land became unclean), lest the land vomit you out when you make it unclean, as it vomited out the nation that was before you. For everyone who does any of these abominations, the persons who do them shall be cut off from among their people."* **Verses 27 – 29 ESV**

God is not happy with immorality. He seeks holiness, and he seeks a people whose desire is to be holy as He is holy. Never allow a feeling of liberality to be part of your lifestyle.

Now Jesus does give freedom from the Law: *"There is therefore now no condemnation to those who are in Christ Jesus, who do not walk according to the flesh, but according to the Spirit. For the law of the Spirit of life in Christ Jesus has made me free from the law of sin and death.* **Romans 8:1 & 2 NKJV**.

In **2 Corinthians 3:17:** *"Now the Lord is the Spirit; and where the Spirit of the Lord is, there is liberty."* **NKJV**.

This freedom and liberty that the believer has is free to do the will of God and not be bound to the will of Satan. We can either be slaves to Satan or slaves to God. The choice is yours.

Romans 6:16: *"Do you not know that when you offer yourselves to someone as obedient slaves, you are slaves of that one you obey—whether you are slaves to sin, which leads to death, or to obedience, which leads to righteousness?"* **NLT.**

Chapter 19

God and Neighbors

God continues with His laws dealing with moral and civil acts as well as laws for pure worship.

The basic rule is to love God and love others; upon these two commandments all the others hang. This was the answer of Jesus when asked the question as to which was the greatest commandment. **Matthew 22:35 – 40; Mark 12:28 – 34 & Luke 10:27**.

God gives a brief review of His commandments here:

- Believers are to be holy as God is holy. **Verse 2**
- Believers are to respect their parents. **Verse 3**
- Believers are to respect and observe the Sabbath. **Verse 3**
- Believers are care for their land and others. **Verses 9 & 10**
- Believers are not to steal. **Verse 11**
- Believers are not to use God's name in vain. **Verse 12**
- Believers are not to cheat but to be fair in all things. **Verse 13**
- Believers are not to make fun of the disadvantaged. **Verse 14**
- Believers are not to participate in the injustice of anyone. **Verse 15**
- Believers are not to spread gossip or bad news about others. **Verse 16**
- Believers are not to hate anyone. **Verse 17**

- Believers are never to take out vengeance upon anyone. **Verse 18**. Believers are to keep their animals pure breeds. **Verse 19**
- Believers are to be pure in their sexual life. **Verse 20**
- Believers are to confess all sins quickly. They are to bring the appropriate sacrifice for that sin, and it must be made according to the regulations of the law. **Verses 21 & 22**
- Believers are to care for the land; it is the duty of all who own land. **Verses 23 – 25**

God gives a stark warning to the people. Worship is to be pure and holy worship; and they are never to take part of any pagan worship ritual, even in the smallest degree. They are never to allow temple prostitution, maiming the body, witchcraft, or to have body markings. **Verses 26 – 29**.

Now God reminds the people of pure, reverent, and consistent worship. They are to reject any act of demon worship. **Verse 31**.

- They are to have great respect for the elderly. **Verse 32**

- They are to be honest in all their business dealings. **Verses 35 & 36**

- They are to adhere to all that God demands. **Verse 37**

Chapter 20

Be Holy for God is Holy

God is holy, and worshippers of a holy God must reflect holiness in their worship. It is shocking, but child sacrifice was part of the worship practice of the Canaanite people. But in a way, child sacrifice is still part of some parents' lives today. One may ask, How is that true?

There are many people who are actually sacrificing their children to the whims and demands of society today. Today, parents seem not to have given the wellbeing of their children a major priority. It seems as though many parents today have no concern for the <u>future of their children</u>. They give children little or no direction in life; and it seems as though their only concern is for <u>their</u> present desires of life. Parents with this mind-set might as well place the child's body on the burning altar of personal desire.

What does God say here?

God says we should be holy, and any act of human sacrifice will be met with the swift judgment and wrath of God. God will cut them off because they have profaned his holy name. **Verse 3**.

Some people may ask: What about God having Abraham sacrifice Isaac? God was testing the faith of Abraham in **Genesis 22**. Abraham was confused because it seemed as though God was asking him to be like the people in the land in which he lived; but God never had the desire for Isaac to be sacrificed. Abraham answered the question of Isaac about the lamb: *"God will provide Himself a Lamb."* **Genesis 22:8 & 12 – 14**. Be certain of this, God never does anything that would go against His holy Word, or against His holy character.

The next warning was to have nothing to do with mediums, psychics, or demon worshipers. The future is in the hands of God; He holds the future, and He holds the hand of His children. Trust God for the future, rest in God for the future, and stay with God as you live out your present life. Do good now. Today is the day to trust in God; so leave the future to God, and obey Him today. **Verses 6 – 8**.

God also places great importance upon honoring one's father and mother. To disgrace one's parents is a <u>capital offense</u>. **Verse 9**

God gives His law against adultery. Again, God is holy and His people are to be holy in their living. **Verse 10 - 12**

Homosexual acts are punishable by death. Homosexual acts are an <u>unnatural</u> act, and the Apostle Paul writes that it *"goes against the natural use of men and women."* **Verses 13 & 14; Romans 1:26 & 27**.

Any perverted sexual act is punishable by death. **Verses 15 & 16**.

Any act of incest is punishable by exiling those who have committed such an act, and this act is punishable by death. **Verses 17 – 22**.

All these laws must be closely observed by the children of Israel. God tells Israel that the keeping of His laws will protect the Children of Israel and keep them pure while living among the vile people that inhabit the land of Canaan. **Verses 22 – 24**.

God will use Israel to judge the people of Canaan, and God is removing them from their land.

Finally, all sacrifices must be pure sacrifices. There is no exemption. **Verse 25**.

The major reason for all these laws is holiness: *"You must be holy because I, the Lord, am holy. I have set you apart from all other people to be my very own."* **Verse 26 NLT**.

A repeated warning against using mediums and psychics is given, as well as the sentence for participating with them. The punishment is death. **Verse 27**.

Believers today are not living under the law; they are living under grace. The grace of God is the result of the atoning sacrifice of Jesus. The law displays that it is impossible for a human being to please God by his own efforts. It took the sacrifice of a spotless and holy person to atone for sins.

The Apostle Paul writes in **Acts 5:8 – 11**: *"But God demonstrates His own love toward us, in that while we were still sinners, Christ died for us. Much more then, having now been justified by His blood, we shall be saved from wrath through Him. For if when we were enemies we were reconciled to God through the death of His Son, much more, having been reconciled, we shall be saved by His life. And not only that, but we also rejoice in God through our Lord Jesus Christ, through whom we have now received the reconciliation."* **NKJV**.

God gave His law to display His holiness. He provided for believers His grace and His mercy and displayed His love as a perfect sacrifice for sin to redeem the believing.

God provided what no one could provide, and He gave to the believer what he could not receive on his own. This gift from God is a great blessing, and the wise person will trust in God's free gift of salvation from sin; there is no other way. **Acts 4:12**.

God sent His son to save mankind, not to kill mankind. Dr. Robert Morris said this:

"God doesn't want to kill you. He wants to kill what is killing you: Your selfish thoughts, your selfish desires, and your selfish feelings ... God would love for you to think about yourself as He thinks about you. He would love for you to know what He wants and desires for your life, and He would love for you to know how He feels about you, rather than what the devil tells you that He feels about you." **Robert Morris.**

God expresses His desire for His priests to be holy as He is holy. God wants those who serve Him in an area of leadership to be holy.

Be careful to live and worship God with a pure heart.

Chapter 21

Holiness

The position of the priest was a special one; it was like no other. The priesthood was selected by God to be a special representative, go-between, and lawyer between the Great and Righteous Judge, God Almighty, and themselves.

There was much expected of him, and he had been given special responsibility by God. The priest was to represent Holy God and sinful man.

Jesus, in His parable of the Faithful and the Evil Servant, responded to Peter: *"Blessed is that servant whom his master will find so doing when he comes"* and *"...For everyone to whom much is given, from him much will be required; and to whom much has been committed, of him they will ask the more."* **Luke 12:43 & 48 NKJV**.

The Tribe of Levi was the selected tribe from which all priests would come; the Tribe of Levi was the family line of Aaron. Aaron was the first high priest, and his sons were the first assistants of the high priest.

There was nothing special or holy about Aaron, but what was special and holy was the calling by God. Being called by God meant that there would be special expectations. We see many of these requirements in **Chapters 8 – 10**. Here, more requirements and expectations are made known.

Today, there is no special people from whom God calls His ministers. God calls those whom He chooses; and He prepares them, He supplies them, and He empowers them to do the calling in which He called them to do.

However, here in Leviticus we see exampled the reverence to duty that God expects of His called ones. By the deaths of Aaron's two oldest sons, Nadab and Abihu, we see the severity of punishment that can be imposed upon the minister of God who takes his duties lightly.

Nadab and Abihu were killed by God for using or bringing *"strange fire"* before holy God. One might say, using strange, or a different kind of fire, doesn't seem to be such a bad thing. I guess Nadab and Abihu may have had that same thought, but that is not for us to judge. God does not use different, and strange, things. God uses holy things; and His word is holy. Anything less than God's requirement is unacceptable to Him.

God desires His priests to be holy because they represent Him. When a person looks upon a priest of God, he must see pure things; in the same way as God requires something special for an animal to be a sacrifice for sin. The sacrifice must be spotless, without blemish, and set apart for that special offering.

Again, what is holy about Aaron and the Levites is their calling. They would have no land allotted to them when they arrived in the Promised Land, and their only duty, or work that they would do, was to be a priest of God before the people.

There are some very unusual things that would exempt someone from carrying out priestly duties.

The first thing that is mentioned as a disqualification of one being able to carry out priestly duties is <u>touching a dead body</u>. The priest was not to touch a dead person; that would make the priest unclean and unable to perform his priestly duties. The priest represents the living God. The only exception here is his father, mother, brother, or sister. **Verse 3**.

The priest did not bury people; others did that. In **Chapter 10** after Aaron's two sons were suddenly killed by God, God tells Moses to tell Aaron: *Then Moses said to Aaron, "This is what the Lord meant when He said: 'I will show myself holy among those who are near me, I will be glorified before the people.' "* **Leviticus 10:3 NLT**.

At the death of Aaron's two oldest sons, Aaron did not touch the bodies of his sons; and Moses called in two cousins of Nadab and Abihu (Mishael and Elzaphan) to carry out their bodies. **Leviticus 10:4**.

Other things that would disqualify the priest from having priestly duties are: (**Verses 5 – 24**)

- He must not shave his head or trim his beard;

- He must not cut his body as idol worshippers do;

- He must always be holy in everything in which he is involved and treat all people in a holy manner;

- He cannot marry a prostitute, a divorced woman, or a widow; He is to be the husband of one woman, and she must be a virgin;

- He must not be driven by emotion;

- He cannot go to the funeral of his parents while carrying out his duties in the Sanctuary; and
- Physical defects exclude one from carrying out priestly duties in the Sanctuary. **Verses 16 – 24**

All these things display the holy character of God, the holy work of God, and the holy way of God.

Today, we are not under the law but under Grace. The mission for the minister of God today still remains to be holy, for God is holy. **1 Peter 1:13 – 17:** *"Therefore gird up the loins of your mind, be sober, and rest your hope fully upon the grace that is to be brought to you at the revelation of Jesus Christ; as obedient children, not conforming yourselves to the former lusts, as in your ignorance; but <u>as He who called you is holy, you also be holy in all your conduct</u>, because it is written, 'Be holy, for I am holy.' And if you call on the Father, who without partiality judges according to each one's work, <u>conduct yourselves throughout the time of your stay here in fear;</u>"* **NKJV**.

The goal of the minster of God is to be holy, and the aim of the called minister of God is to be daily active in carrying out his calling.

The Apostle Paul encourages the church at Ephesus the last time that he would see them: *"But none of these things move me; nor do I count my life dear to myself, so that I may <u>finish my race with joy, and the ministry which I received from the Lord Jesus, to testify to the gospel of the grace of God.</u>"* **Acts 20:24 NKJV**.

In **1 Corinthians 10:11** we read: *"Now all these things happened to them <u>as examples</u>, and they <u>were written for our admonition, upon whom the ends of the ages have come</u>."* **NKJV**.

We study the Old Testament to get an understanding as to the holiness of God, the weakness of mankind, and the willingness of God to be our great helper.

The aim of the called minster of God is to be holy and obedient to his calling. Yet, in the midst of being what God desires him to be, every minster of God will suffer times of failure. He will be attacked, he will be falsely accused, and he will be discouraged by friends, family, and respected colleagues. Still through all this, God remains faithful. Why would God allow this, one may ask?

David Jeremiah wrote this in a devotional: *"God allows disruptive moments in our life that we almost always question or resist because they are painful, unanticipated, misunderstood, and often not optional. Yet in hindsight, they are always embraced for the good or blessing which results. In the Old Testament, Job is the classic example of a life being disrupted, which Paul's thorn in the flesh is an obvious New Testament example. If God has allowed a disruptive moment in your life, walk through it by faith rather than by sight. Then be prepared to say: 'Now I understand.' "* **David Jeremiah**.

Chapter 22

Acceptable Offerings

Moses continues to give God's instructions for the priesthood to Aaron. Aaron, his sons, and the Levites had a special calling from God. They had a unique mission in life, and with that calling and mission, there was a special responsibility that was beyond God's calling and mission for the ordinary people. God expected more of Aaron, his sons, and the Levites than He did with the rest of the children of Israel, and because of this special expectation, they must be careful to be faithful to that trust. Not to consider their calling and mission sacred and holy would demand a severe punishment.

Jesus mentioned that to whom much was given, much was expected; and God expected much of the priests who led in worship with His people. The priests were to take great care in how they ministered, where they ministered, and when they ministered. Everything must be done in order and with great care to be holy and to direct all praise and glory to God alone.

They were not to lead in worship if they were sick, if they had come into contact with anything unholy, or if they had any reason to be seen as less than holy in any way. *". . . that they abstain from the holy things of the people of Israel, which they dedicate to me, so that they do not profane my holy name: I am the Lord. Say to them, 'If any one of all your offspring throughout your generations approaches the holy things that the people of Israel dedicate to the Lord, while he has an uncleanness, that person shall be cut off from my presence: I am the Lord.'* "**Verses 2 – 3 ESV**. We see the danger and judgment of unholy service with the act of Aaron's two oldest sons, Nadab and Abihu. **Leviticus 10**.

What does that say to us today? It says that anyone who is involved in ministry should take great care that what he does for the Lord, where he is serving the Lord, and when he is serving the Lord is always God honoring, God glorifying, and God loving. Great care must be taken as a believer serves the Lord! Never do things your way; always do things God's way. As you serve God, those that you are ministering to must see Jesus and not you.

The Apostle Paul writes that sin is falling short of the glory of God in **Romans 3:23**; and for any servant of God to do anything that might bring glory to himself, it is falling short of the glory of God and, therefore, that is sin.

In all that we do in word or deed, it must be for the glory of God. **1 Corinthians 10:31:** *"Therefore, whether you eat or drink, or whatever you do, do all to the glory of God."* **NKJV**.

As the priests were to be careful to glorify God at all times, so too the believer today must be careful to glorify God at all times. Never desire to do things your way; always seek to do all things in God's way.

All believers today, the followers of Christ Jesus, are viewed by God as His priests. The Apostle Peter writes in **1 Peter 2:9:** *"But you are a chosen generation, a royal priesthood, a holy nation, His own special people, that you may proclaim the praises of Him who called you out of darkness into His marvelous light."* **NKJV**.

God warns against voluntarily doing things out of pride and pleasure, but He also points out that there will be times that a priest will *"unintentionally"* do something that was wrong, and if so, the offender must pay, or repay, for his offense. **Verses 14 - 16:** *"And if anyone eats of a holy thing unintentionally, he* *shall <u>add the fifth of its value to it and give the holy thing to the priest</u>. They shall not profane the holy things of the people of Israel, which they contribute to the Lord, and so cause them to bear iniquity and guilt, by eating their holy things: for I am the Lord who sanctifies them."* **ESV**.

Notice that even an <u>unintentional</u> offense can cause others to sin; they may consider that unintentional offense to be okay and then <u>intentionally</u> do what the first believer has done "<u>unintentionally.</u>" When a believer realizes that he has committed an unintentional and outward sin that was witnessed by others, it must be confessed publicly; not only to God, but before others. Like the saying today goes: "Man-up."

Not only is the priest to live a holy and acceptable life before all people, but he is especially to be mindful as he makes holy and acceptable offerings to God for the people and himself. The offering must be acceptable, by being exactly what God has desired.

Never feel that "God will understand" or God will excuse our sin; He will not. God cannot even look upon disobedience and sin because He has holy eyes. God expects all believers to be obedient. We see things through sinful eyes; God sees things through holy eyes.

 Let me inject something here. What does God desire? God desires obedience and holiness, but He makes provisions for disobedience and sin. Remember what Samuel told King Saul when Saul disobeyed the command of God? *"Has the Lord as great delight in burnt offerings and sacrifices, as in obeying the voice of the Lord? <u>Behold, to obey is better than sacrifice, and to heed than the fat of rams</u>."* **1 Samuel 15:22 NKJV**.

I have heard people say: *"Forgiveness is easier to get than permission."* That is not a pattern in which a true believer is to live his life. That is saying, I can sin and then just ask God for forgiveness. Such a mindset exposes the inward heart of a man. It shouts to others that he is not genuinely saved; that man is a liar and is not a child of God.

We know that the desire of God is that all men would be saved:

2 Peter 3:9: *"The Lord is not slack concerning His promise, as some count slackness, but is longsuffering toward us, not willing that any should perish but that all should come to repentance."* **NKJV**.

1 Timothy 2:4: *"Who desires all men to be saved and to come to the knowledge of the truth."* **NKJV**.

However, all men <u>will not be saved</u>; most will freely choose not to believe God, and they must pay the penalty for their sin. In the same light, God <u>desires for all believers not to sin</u>; but all believers will sin, because mankind is born into sin. All have sinned and fallen short of the glory of God. **Romans 3:23**.

1 John 1: 8 - 2:1 & 2: *"<u>If we say that we have no sin, we deceive ourselves, and the truth is not in us</u>. <u>If we confess our sins</u>, He is faithful and just to forgive us our sins and to cleanse us from all unrighteousness. <u>If we say that we have not sinned</u>, <u>we make Him a liar, and His word is not in us</u>. My little children, these things I write to you , so that you may not sin. And if anyone sins, we have an Advocate with the Father, Jesus Christ the righteous. And He Himself is the propitiation for our sins, and not for ours only but also for the whole world."* **NKJV**

1 John 3:4 – 9: *"Whoever commits sin also commits lawlessness, and sin is lawlessness. . . Little children, let no one deceive you, He who <u>practices righteousness is righteous, just as He is righteous</u>. He who sins is of the devil, for the devil has sinned from the beginning. For this purpose, the Son of God was manifested, that He might destroy the works of the devil. Whoever is born of God does not sin, for His seed remains in him; and he cannot sin, <u>because he has been born of God</u>."* **NKJV**.

The purification of sin has been made by the holy implanting of The Seed of Righteousness of Jesus Christ into the believer. That purification and atonement for sin is the righteousness of Jesus being poured out by the Father upon the new creations of God.

2 Corinthians 5:21: *"For He made Him who knew no sin to be sin for us, that we might become the righteousness of God in Him."* **NKJV.**

2 Corinthians 5:17: *"Therefore, if anyone is in Christ, he is a new creation; old things have passed away; behold, all things have become new."* **NKJV**.

So in order for the sacrifice for sin to be acceptable to God, the sacrifice must be pure, the act of carrying out that sacrifice must be pure, and the person who is leading in the worship act must be pure. All things must be done as God expects.

"So you shall keep my commandments and do them: I am the Lord. And you shall not profane my holy name, that I may be sanctified among the people of Israel. I am the Lord who sanctifies you, who brought you out of the land of Egypt to be your God: I am the Lord." **Verse 31 ESV.**

All things that are done in worship must be pure, they must be obeyed, and they must be honoring to God. Make sure your life is honoring to God!

Think about these words by the Gospel songwriter Steve Green:

Touch Your People Once Again

"We need wisdom, we need power,

and true love for each other;

We have had so many big but empty words.

So we come before Your face,

Asking for Your grace;

Bring Your people to a state of kingdom life.

Restore your church again.

Touch Your people once again,

With Your precious holy hand, we pray;

Let Your kingdom shine upon this earth,

Through a living glorious church;

Not for temporary deeds,

But to restored authority and power,

Let a mighty rushing wind blow in;

Touch Your people once again.

Lord, You see Your tired servants,

Your broken wounded soldiers;

Oh how much we need your precious healing hand.

We need the power of the cross as the only source for us,

When we stand up facing final battle cry;

Restore Your church again.

Steve Green

Yes, do things God's way and you will honor Him, serve others, feel blessed by God, and receive a reward from His good hand.

Chapter 23

Feasts

Now God gives to Aaron His directions in how to observe the various festivals for worship, or those special appointed and holy times of assembly for worship. There are seven special days and feast days:

1. **The Sabbath**, **Verse 3:** The Sabbath is a holy "Day of Rest;" it is observed weekly. The Sabbath was made for man. Jesus said in **Mark 2:27 & 28**: *"And He said to them, 'The Sabbath was made for man, and not man for the Sabbath. Therefore the Son of Man is also Lord of the Sabbath.' "* **NKJV**.

   On the seventh day of creation, God rested from His work, as we read in **Genesis 2:2**. Believers do not worship on the seventh day of the week, Saturday, but on the first day of the week, Sunday, the reason being that Jesus arose on the first day of the week. The Apostle Paul writes of the collection of financial support for his ministry to be collected on the first day of the week in **1 Corinthians 16:2**. We also read of this gathering of believers on the first day of the week in **Acts 20:7**. The term, "The Lord's Day," is only found one time in Scripture: **Revelation 1:10**, the Apostle John writes, *"I was in the Spirit on <u>the Lord's Day</u>, and I heard behind me a loud voice, as of a trumpet,"* **NKJV**.

   The day is not as significant as is the time for rest. God commanded that man is to *"Remember the Sabbath day to keep it holy."* **Exodus 20:8 – 11**. Not to have a day of rest, or Sabbath, is a sin; it is to disobey one of the ten commandments. To disobey this commandment is as much of a sin as any other: slandering God and His name, worshiping idols, to murder, to commit adultery, to covet, to steal, to dishonor one's parents, or to lie. Remember the Sabbath to keep it holy! Have a day of rest and worship!

2. **The Passover and Unleavened Bread, Verses 4 – 8:** Passover is celebrated on the Jewish month of <u>Nisan 14 & 15</u>, around our calendar month of March and June. It is called Passover in remembrance of the tenth plague in Egypt, as the death angel passed over the homes of the Jews who had the blood of a lamb painted on the lintel and door posts of their home. **Exodus 12**.

   Believers today celebrate this as Easter, in remembrance of the blood of Jesus being spilt for their sins. Jesus was the Passover Lamb, The Lamb of God. The Apostle John writes in **Revelation 5:6 – 10**: *". . . And I looked, and behold, in the midst of the throne and of the four living creatures, and in the midst of the elders, <u>stood a Lamb as though it had been slain,</u> . . . ."*

   Jesus is the Passover Lamb of God, and His blood brings life, eternal life. Jesus is the final sacrifice for sin. **Hebrews 10:12**: *"But this Man, after He had offered one sacrifice for sins forever, sat down at the right hand of God."* **NKJV**.

3. **The Feast of Unleavened Bread, Verses 6 – 8:** This feast is celebrated with the Passover. It is celebrated on the day after Passover. The Feast of Unleavened Bread is also a day of rest. This is somewhat a day of fasting where God's children can turn their eyes upon the goodness of God in their lives.

4. **The Feast of First Fruits, Verses 9 – 14:** This feast follows Passover and Unleavened Bread. It is in remembrance of the provisions of God as they entered into the Promised land. A celebration day that believers observe that is similar is Thanksgiving Day.

5. **The Feast of Weeks, Pentecost, Verses 15 – 22:** Pentecost comes 50 days after Passover. Pentecost is also the day that the Holy Spirit came upon the believers. Luke documented this in **Acts 2:1 – 4:** *"When <u>the Day of Pentecost had fully come</u>, they were all with one accord in one place. . . . And they were all filled with the Holy Spirit and began to speak with other tongues, as the Spirit gave them utterance."* **NKJV**. Pentecost is observed on the 6th or 7th day of the Jewish month of Sivan, around our months of May and June.

6. **The Feast of Trumpets, Verses 23 – 25:** The Feast of Trumpets is in recognition of the coming of a new year, held on the Jewish Tishri or our month of September and October. It is called Rosh Hashanah. On this day, the people were to remember the mercies of God. This feast day could be compared with our New Year's Eve.

7. **The Day of Atonement, Verses 26 – 32:** Also known as Yom Kippur. It was a day of fasting, prayer, and worship. It is celebrated on the 10th day of the Jewish month of Tishri or our month of October. This is the Jewish New Year and follows The Feast of Trumpets. For the believer, Jesus is our Atonement and the Giver of new life in Christ Jesus; the believer is given a new spiritual body for eternity.

8. **The Feast of Booths or Tabernacles, Verses 33 - 44:** This feast is celebrated in the Jewish month of Tishri,

or our month of October. The Festival of Booths or Tabernacles is also known as Sukkot. This festival is also a time of celebration for the good hand of God upon the lives of believers for His provisions and protection.

Chapter 24

Care for Furnishing

Here in Chapter 25 God gives to Moses His instructions to give to Aaron concerning how the priests are to care for the holy furnishing in His Tabernacle. Remember, God is holy, His name is holy, His place for worship, the Tabernacle, was holy, and what was inside the Tabernacle was holy as well. The priests were His holy representatives; and as His holy representatives they must take great care in their duties, in themselves, and in the maintaining of the holy furnishings inside the holy Tabernacle.

If great care is not taken, God will also distribute His holy judgment for any unholy thing, any unholy attitude, and any unholy deed. The writer of Hebrews points out that it is a <u>fearful thing to fall into the hands of a living and holy God</u>, **Hebrews 10:31**.

- <u>The Lamps</u>, **Verses 5 – 9**: The light from the Golden Candlestand is to be an eternal flame. The light for the oil in the lampstand came from a flame taken from the Altar of Sacrifice; and the priest is to take special care and make careful provision for the special holy oil to be on hand. The Golden Lampstand was located inside the Holy Place and before the veil that separated the Holy Place from the Most Holy Place. *"Aaron shall arrange it from evening to morning before the Lord regularly. It shall be a statute forever throughout your* *generations. He shall arrange the lamps on the lampstand of pure gold before the Lord regularly."* **Verses 3 & 4 ESV**.

Like the Lampstand, Jesus is the Light of the world. Jesus is the <u>everlasting light of the world</u>. His light never dims or goes out; His light beams brightly to the world eternally.

- <u>The Bread</u>, **Verses 10 – 16**: The bread was prepared weekly and was placed upon the Golden Table inside the Holy Place; the old loaves were replaced by the priest weekly with new loaves. There were 12 loaves that were stacked in 2 rows. The old loaves were to be eaten by the priest inside the Holy Place each week.

  Jesus is the everlasting Bread of Life, **John 6:51**; Jesus is also the sustainer of life, and there is no need of replacing Him. Jesus sustains believers eternally. Jesus is also the Great High Priest of all believers, as we read in **Hebrews 8:1 – 6**: *"Now this is the main point of the things we are saying: We have such a High Priest, who is seated at the right hand of the throne of the Majesty in the heavens, a Minister of the sanctuary and of the true tabernacle which the Lord erected, and not man . . . But now He has obtained a more excellent ministry, inasmuch as he is also Mediator of a better covenant, which was established on better promises."* **NKJV**. Also read in **Hebrews 4:11 – 14; & 7:11 – 28**.

God is God, and He must be worshiped as God and as the only God. God is holy and He is to be revered. To blaspheme the holy name of God and the holiness of God demands godly punishment. There is an instance given of such irreverence to the holy name of God, and it was punishable by death. God's punishment is witnessed here in **Verses 17 – 23**.

Men do not judge; God judges. We read that vengeance belongs to God alone, **Romans 12:19**. God's appointed arm of judgment on earth is His appointed authorities. He appoints governments to carry out His judgment, but man is not the judge. Man judges by the principles set forth by God.

The appointed dispenser of judgment is government. Paul writes of this in **Romans 13:1 – 7**: *"Let every soul be subject to the governing authorities. <u>For there is no authority except from God, and the authorities that exist are appointed by God</u>. . . <u>he is God's minister, an avenger to execute wrath on him who practices evil</u>. . . ."* **NKJV**. Government is God's present arm of justice, but eternal justice will come at the end of time.

God the Father is the Great Judge, and final Judge of all. In **Revelation 22:11 – 15** is recorded the Great White Throne Judgment.

The person who is judged here for blasphemy in **Verses 10 – 23** is a man whose mother was a Hebrew from the tribe of Dan, and his father was an Egyptian.

The crime was blaspheming the holy name of God. Today, the holy name of God is used so flippantly and disrespectfully. God is holy and His name is holy! Sadly, we hear the name of God angerly unleashed upon others for anything and everything. We hear the plea of all types of people asking God to damn someone or something to death and destruction for some deed that was not pleasing to them, while all the time they are not living a life that is pleasing to God. I shudder when I hear such things, and I shudder a lot! It is sad to say but such blasphemy is a common and everyday thing. Do not be included with such blasphemers!

The penalty that was demanded by God was stoning. **Verse 13 – 16**: *"Then the Lord spoke to Moses, saying, "Bring out of the camp the one who cursed, and let all who heard him lay their hands on his head, and let all the congregation stone* *him. And speak to the people of Israel, saying, Whoever curses his God shall bear his sin. Whoever blasphemes the name of the Lord shall surely be put to death. All the congregation shall stone him."* **ESV**.

Always honor God, reverence God, and keep His holy name holy.

With the judgment of God revealed upon the man for blasphemy, God also gives His statutes and his verdicts for other crimes. These judgments are similar to the 282 crimes contained on a Babylonian obelisk dating back to **1754 BC** called *"The Hammurabi Code."* It was a rule of law that demanded *"an eye for an eye, a tooth for a tooth."*

Now, these laws of God given to the children of Israel are not copies of Hammurabi, but they were laws already used by other peoples and nations. When Cain killed his brother Abel, God judged him for his crime. God also judged Sodom and Gomorrah for their crimes and many others.

The principle here is that all judgments and punishments for crimes committed must be appropriate, fitting and just for the crime committed. Also seen here is a warning against being too quick to judge someone, or a rush to judgment. Any rush to judgment endangers one to indict someone with a false judgment. This rushing to judgment is mob rule; and God will punish mob rule.

There are other statutes and laws; and one will see that the punishment for killing an animal is not the same as killing a person. It is not to say that animals are unimportant; they are important. God charged Adam with the responsibility of caring for the animals of the Garden of Eden. Animals are creations of God and must be seen as being God's creation. The punishment for killing an animal is compensation plus an added assessment for it. *"and whoever kills an animal shall restore it; but whoever kills a man shall be put to death."* **Verse 21 NKJV.**

The conclusion of these judgments of God ends with the stoning of the one who blasphemed God's name. **Verse 23:** *"Then Moses spoke to the children of Israel; and they took outside the camp him who had cursed, and stoned him with stones. So the children of Israel did as the Lord commanded Moses."* **NKJV.**

The most fearful thing that will ever be experienced will be at the Great White Throne Judgment at the end of time. To hear the words of the Great Judge Himself personally curse you and say: *". . . Depart from Me, <u>you cursed</u>, into the <u>everlasting fire prepared for the devil and his angels</u>:"* **Matthew 25:41 NKJV.**

Did you notice that hell was not prepared for man? Hell was prepared for Satan and his angels. Those of mankind who are sentenced to spend eternity in the fire of hell go there as intruders.

God sent His only Begotten Son, Jesus Christ, to earth to pay the price for sin, and to give all people the choice of where they will spend eternity. Where will you spend eternity? Will it be eternal life in heaven with God, His angels, and His children; or will it be eternal death in hell with Satan, his angels, and all those who have cursed God by rejecting His gift?

Chapter 25

Sabbath and Jubilee Year

In the giving of the law on Mount Sinai God declared that He alone is God. He demands that He alone is to be worshipped; He demands that His name is to be revered as holy; and He commands that the seventh day of the week is to be a holy rest for mankind.

At the conclusion of God's work in the creation week, God rested, or He finished His work and ceased from work. In **Genesis 1:31 – 2:3** we read: *"Then God saw everything that He had made, and indeed it was very good. So the evening and the morning were the sixth day. Thus the heavens and the earth, and all the host of them, were finished. <u>And on the seventh day God ended His work which He had done. The God blessed the seventh day and sanctified it</u>, because in it He rested from all His work which God had created and made."* **NKJV**.

The Sabbath is not only to be kept, it is to be esteemed as holy. Do you have a holy day of rest? If not, you are disobeying God.

Notice that not only is mankind to rest, but the land, the animals, and all of creation is to have a rest. **Verses 2 – 4**: *"... When you come into the land that I give you, <u>the land shall keep a Sabbath to the Lord. For six years you shall sow your field, and for six years you shall prune your vineyard and gather in its fruits, but in the seventh year there shall be a Sabbath of solemn rest for the land, a Sabbath to the Lord.</u> . . ."* **ESV**.

After six years of labor and working their land, they must allow the land to rest. During that seventh year, they were to eat off the land, but not harvest the land. The seventh year was given to the Lord, and the Lord would sustain them with the fruit and grain that would come up voluntarily that year. **Verses 5 -7**.

This godly provision would be more than enough to sustain them and the animals. There was no need for worry or concern in this seventh year of rest. As Jesus noted that God cares for the birds of the air, He also cares for us. **Matthew 6:26**.

The voluntary produce of the land would not only feed and sustain the people but it would sustain the animals as well. **Verses 6 & 7**:   *"The Sabbath of the land shall provide food for you, for yourself and for your male and female slaves and for your hired worker and the sojourner who lives with you, and for your cattle and for the wild animals that are in your land: all its yield shall be for food."* **ESV**

Not only was there to be a seventh day Sabbath of rest for the people, and a seven year Sabbath for the land, but there was to be a seventh decade Sabbath which was called <u>The Year of Jubilee.</u> **Verses 8 – 22**.

This Year of Jubilee that occurred every 50 years was a reset; it was a redemption of the land, a redemption of slaves, and a redemption of anything that was sold over the past 50 years because of some adverse circumstance.

The Year of Jubilee began on the fiftieth year. It was trumpeted on the tenth day of the seventh month of the 49th year, which was the month of <u>Tishi;</u> and it was the Day of Atonement. The Jewish name is <u>Rosh Hashanah</u>. It was the new year's eve of the new year. The sound of the Shofar, or trumpet, was sounded loudly to bring in this Year of Jubilee. **Verses 8 – 10:** *"You shall count seven weeks of years, seven* *times seven years, so that the time of the seven weeks of years shall give you forty-nine years. Then you shall sound the loud trumpet on the tenth day of the seventh month. On the Day of Atonement you shall sound the trumpet throughout all your land. And you shall consecrate the fiftieth year, and proclaim liberty throughout the land to all its inhabitants. It shall be a jubilee for you, when each of you shall return to his property and each of you shall return to his clan."* **ESV**.

During this 50th year all debts are canceled, and lands that have been sold were restored to the original owner and freedom was proclaimed throughout the land. **Verse 10**. Verse 10 is inscribed on the Liberty Bell: *"proclaim liberty throughout all the land unto all the inhabitants thereof."*

What is seen in this chapter is redemption. Redemption is the crimson thread that is seen all throughout Scripture, and Jesus Christ is The Redeemer, Who paid in full the required redemption price for all who would believe in Him. Jesus is the restorer of mankind and all creation.

Right now God is preparing a new Heaven, a new Earth and a new Jerusalem for worship for His redeemed children. John the Beloved writes of this total restoration and eternal Jubilee in **Revelation 21**.

In **Verses 23 – 55** we see the redemption of not only land and property, but redemption of people from slavery. Now, God does not approve of slavery any more than He approves of any other sin. Slavery happens because of sin, and we live in a world of sin. We are born into this world of sin with a sinful nature. Mankind is not basically good; he is basically bad. Jesus came to give mankind a <u>new nature, to make him a new creation.</u> **2 Corinthians 5:17**.

The reason for redemption is slavery. Again, Scripture does not approve of slavery, but slavery is part of this earth's system, and that system is sin. Satan enslaves, and unredeemed mankind lives in that system of slavery.

We know that some of the Children of Israel owned slaves; and we know that there were some in the early church who owned slaves as well, such as Philemon and his slave Onesimus, recorded in the Apostle Paul's letter to **Philemon**.

God does not desire for anyone to sin, but they will sin because we live in a world of sin and are born into sin as a slave to sin. **Romans 3:23** & **1 John 1:8 – 2:2**.

The Apostle Paul writes in **Romans 6:16**: *"Do you not know that to whom you present yourselves slaves to obey, you are that one's slaves whom you obey whether of sin leading to death or of obedience leading to righteousness?"* **NKJV**.

Many times in the letters of Paul, he refers to himself as a bond-slave of Christ Jesus, as do others. **1 Corinthians 7:20 – 24, Titus 1:1; James 1:1; 2 Peter 1:1, & Jude 1**.

Slavery will continue all throughout time. It will never be eliminated. Slaves are not their own; Paul tells us that we are not our own but we were bought with a price in **1 Corinthians 6:20**.

Slavery is not the greatest sin; the greatest sin of all <u>is the rejection of God's Only Begotten Son, Jesus Christ, The Redeemer</u>.

The enemy of mankind is Satan and his buddies. Scripture refers to them as the principalities and powers, the workers of iniquity in heavenly places. **Ephesians 6:12**. The only way to defeat Satan is to resist him by drawing near to God, and then God will draw near to you. **James 4:7 – 10**.

We read of the redemption of Ruth in **Ruth 3 & 4** by Boaz, who was her kinsman redeemer, or her close relative. *"And the close relative said, 'I cannot redeem it for myself, lest I ruin my own inheritance. You redeem my right of redemption for* *yourself, for I cannot redeem it.' "* **Ruth 4:6 NKJV**. The closest kin of Naomi and her daughter-in-law Ruth was willing to redeem but he was not able to redeem Naomi and Ruth. However, Boaz was the next nearest kinsman, and he was both able to redeem and willing to redeem.

Someone has noted this of Boaz as a redeemer. He was:

1. <u>Qualified</u> to legally redeem, **Ruth 3:9**

2. <u>Able</u> to financially redeem, **Ruth 3:12**

3. <u>Desired</u> to redeem, **Ruth 3:13**

4. <u>Carried out his desire</u> to redeem, **Ruth 3:9**.

In order for redemption to take place all four of these factors must be true. **4:1 – 10**.

Jesus carried out all of these and that made Him the Redeemer of all believers. **John 3:16**.

Chapter 26

Blessings for Obedience

To obey God brings blessing, success, and joy in life; but to disobey God guarantees failure, disappointment, and punishment.

The prophet Samuel told the disobedient king Saul that his sacrifices were of no value to God. God desires obedience more than sacrifice, as we read in **1 Samuel 15:22**: *"But Samuel replied, 'What is more pleasing to the Lord: your burnt offerings and sacrifices or your obedience to his voice? Obedience is far better than sacrifice. Listening to Him is much better than offering the fat of rams. Rebellion is as bad as the sin of witchcraft, and stubbornness is as bad a worshiping idols. So because you have rejected the word of the Lord, he has rejected you from being king."* **NLT**.

The Children of Israel had two besetting sins that so easily overtook them, which were the sin of mummering and the sin of idolatry. They voiced their love, devotion, and worship to God but acted out the evil of their heart. The Children of Israel would suffer many unnecessary evils because of presumptuous sins, rebellion, and stubbornness. They were filled with envy, wrath, greed, covetousness, and pride. They wanted things done their way, not God's way. They robbed God, thought they were wiser than God, and they angered God. Do you know people like that? I do.

In this very chapter we see the reason for Israel's punishment as a nation throughout their history. God promised blessing for obedience. God desired His name to be honored and His holiness to be observed and worshipped. All idols of false gods were banned, **Verse 1**; He desired for the Sabbath to be observed, **Verse 2**; He desired for his commandments and laws to be obeyed, **Verse 3**.

If they obeyed and did all these requirements of God, He promised blessing:

- A fruitful land and abundance of crops; a land flowing with milk and honey. **Verses 4, 5, & 9 – 11**

- A life filled with peace, contentment, and lived with no cause for fear. **Verses 6, 11 – 13**

- A life that would be revered, envied and feared by their enemies; and they would easily dominate any foe. **Verse 7.**

If they disobeyed and rebelled against God and His commandments, they could expect the wrath of God. God warns that disobedience guarantees unneeded punishment, such as:

- Sudden and unexpected terror. **Verse 16**

- Continual epidemics of disease. **Verse 16**

- Defeat by their enemies, overcome by unfounded fear, and insecurity in life. **Verse 17**

- Ever increasing and mounting trouble in life, and unanswered prayers. **Verse 18 & 19**

- Hostility from God Himself, and God's presence gone. **Verses 21 – 25**

- Famine in the land. **Verse 26**

- They will do the unthinkable, offer their children as a human sacrifice to the idols of their false gods. **Verses 27 – 32**

- God will bring a deportation of the people to foreign lands and they will be demoralized by the enemy, and many would die in that foreign land. **Verses 33 – 39**.

There is a great truth that is revealed here, and that truth is that if the people would repent of their sins and return to God, He would forgive and heal their land. **Verses 40 – 43; 2 Chronicles 7:14**.

You can rely on this: God is good, unbelievably forgiving, loving, gracious, merciful, longsuffering, and kind. The act of God the Father sending His Only Begotten Son to earth for the sins of the world proves His goodness; and it is mind boggling to me. Who would do such a thing? God the Father would do such a thing. *"For God so loved the world, that He gave His Only Begotten Son."* **John 3:16**; God *"is longsuffering . . . not willing that any should perish."* **2 Peter 3:9 NKJV**.

We have listed here why Israel would suffer in the future. God came very close to totally wiping them out.

What does that say to us today? It says that God has made a way for escape, for repentance, and for forgiveness. The Apostle Paul writes in **Romans 5:6 – 11:** *"For when we were still without strength, in due time Christ died for the ungodly. . . . God demonstrates His own love toward us, in that while we were still sinners, Christ died for us. . . . we also rejoice in God through our Lord Jesus Christ, through whom we have now received the reconciliation."* **NKJV**.

That is much too marvelous to understand. We must believe it. Why would a pure and holy God come to live among such a depraved, unthankful, and unlovable people? He came because of His great love.

Think about that, let that thought sink in, and then fall on your knees and praise this glorious One for what He has done for you!

Chapter 27

Making Vows

This chapter of Leviticus is thought by some to have been added to the book of Leviticus later on in the history of Israel by some other inspired person.

In this chapter God gives His requirements for applying value to various items of property that have been dedicated to God, specifically voluntary vows that had been made by the people who had donated various things for the construction of the Tabernacle.

These voluntary vows and pledges have been made holy by the very purpose for which they were vowed and pledged. The people gave gold, silver, jewelry, animals, and later would give land holdings. There were tithes to the Tabernacle to be used in worship and support of the priesthood. Values are given for all things that had been given to be used in the giving of tithes and offerings.

First of all, there is a value of people who have been dedicated to the Lord, such as Samuel was dedicated to the Lord by his mother Hannah. **1 Samuel 1:11**: *"Then she made a vow and said, 'O Lord of hosts, if You will indeed look on the affliction of Your maidservant and remember me, and not forget Your maidservant, but will give Your maidservant a male child, <u>then I will give him to the Lord all the days of his life, and no razor shall come upon his head.</u>'"* **NKJV**.

The important thing to remember here is that these vows were voluntary, and many times they were given for a specific amount of time. There is another reason for placing value on individuals who have been dedicated to God, and that was to redeem them with a substitute payment.

We see here a difference in value as to age and gender. Why the difference? Perhaps it was because of the ability of a person to work, their various skills, and how hard they were able to work. We see in **Verse 3** that the redemption price for a <u>20 – 60 year old man</u> was 50 shekels of silver, which was equivalent to about 50 months' wages. This would cause a person to think twice if he desired to take back his vow.

The redemption price for property was its calculated value in relation to the Year of Jubilee + 20%. Jesus condemned the Pharisees for falsely saying that their fathers and mothers were of no value to them because they were a gift to God. **Mark 7:11 – 13**; **Verses 16 – 27**.

All these valuations are for the glory of God and not mankind. All things in actuality belong to God, the Creator of all.

What is meant by redeeming his tithes? **Verses 30 – 33**. Perhaps a person might have some dire need, such as needing money to buy seed for growing a crop. This was like borrowing money for one's livelihood; but when the harvest came, the tithe was to be repaid, plus a 20% addition of value that must be paid. **Verses 30 – 33**.

The major thing here is being honest with God, and in doing so, God will be gracious to you.

Conversations

On

The Books of

Numbers

By

Danny Glenn Thomas

Just for the Basics Series

Table of Contents

Foreword

Paul tells Timothy in **2 Timothy 2:15:** *"Be diligent to present yourself approved to God, a worker who does not need to be ashamed, rightly dividing the word of truth."* **NKJV**. The **King James Version** renders this verse: *"Study to show thyself approved unto God, a workman that needeth not to be ashamed, rightly dividing the word of truth."* The **New Living Translation** has stated it this way: *"Work hard so you can present yourself to God and receive his approval. Be a good worker, one who does not need to be ashamed and who correctly explains the word of truth."* Eugene Peterson in his paraphrase, **The Message,** writes: *"Concentrate on doing your best for God, work you won't be ashamed of, laying out the truth plain and simple."*

This is what I have set out to do. I am presenting a plain, simple, and basic commentary on the Word of God. I want to present the Word, compared by the Word, with the hope of creating a greater desire of the reader to want to know more and to seek to go deeper into God's Word.

I found written in the front of my Dad's first preaching Bible this statement: *"The task of the scholar is to guarantee the purity of the text; to get as close as possible to the Word as originally given. He may compare Scripture with Scripture until he discovers the true meaning of the text. But right there, his authority ends. He must never sit in judgment upon what is written; he must not bring the meaning of the Word before the bar of his reason."* I do not know the source of this statement, but it is true, and that is my desire as I write this series of commentaries or expositions on Scripture.

Introduction to Numbers

The book of Numbers is the fourth book of Moses; and it covers the forty-year wandering of Israel in the wilderness, the influence that some of the nations had upon Israel, and concludes with them ready to enter the promised land.

This fourth book of Moses is called Numbers because of the two censuses that were taken of the people 20 years old and older. The purpose for the census was for it to be used in preparing an army for war. The first census was taken at Sinai, as they began their 40-year trek in the wilderness, and the second was in Moab after the plague sent from God upon Israel for their idol worship with Baal of Peor in **Chapter 25**.

Numbers can be divided into three sections:

1. Israel in the wilderness. 1 – 22
2. The foreign influence of the nations. 22 – 25
3. Preparation for entering the Promised Land. 26 – 36

Dr. Douglas K. Wilson Jr, one time pastor of the First Baptist Church of Orchard Park Church, Orchard Park, New York, had a unique outline of Numbers presented in The Holman Illustrated Bible Dictionary:

1. Heading out from Sinai. 1 – 10
2. Heading nowhere at Kadesh-Barnea. 11 – 21
3. Heading into Trouble. 22 – 25
4. Heading for the Promised Land. 26 – 36

I tend to like this outline.

The wandering began around 1444 BC and concluded around 1406 BC. During this unnecessary wandering the Children of Israel tested the patience of God. We read in **Acts**

3:20 – 28 where Stephen reviewed the history of Israel with the religious leaders of his day, just before he was stoned.

The Apostle Paul reviewed the wanderings in **1 Corinthians 10:1 – 12:** *"Moreover, brethren, I do not want you to be unaware that all our fathers were under the cloud, all passed through the sea, . . . <u>Now all these things happened to them as examples, and they were written for our admonition,</u> upon whom the ends of the ages have come. Therefore let him who thinks he stands take heed lest he fall."* **NKJV**; and also the writer of Hebrews writes in **Hebrews 11:23 – 29:** *"By faith Moses, . . . refused to be called the son of Pharaoh's daughter, . . . kept the Passover . . . passed through the Red Sea . . . ."* **NKJV**.

Chapter 1

The First Census

"Take a census," God says. What is the purpose for this census? The reason is to prepare for war. All the fighting men 20 years of age and older were numbered. **Verse 2:** *"Take a census of all the congregation of the people of Israel, <u>by clans</u>, by fathers' houses, according to the number of names, <u>every male, head by head. From twenty years old and upward</u>, all in Israel who are able to go to war, <u>you and Aaron shall list them</u>, company by company. <u>And there shall be with you a man from each tribe</u>, each man being the head of the house of his fathers. And these are the names of the men who <u>shall assist you</u>."* **ESV**

King David conducted a similar census which is recorded in **2 Samuel 24:1 – 6 & 1 Chronicles 21:1 – 6**.

We read in **Verses 47 – 54** that the tribe of Levi was exempt from military service because they were responsible for protecting the Tabernacle: *"Only the tribe of <u>Levi you shall not list, and you shall not take a census of them</u> . . . But <u>appoint the Levites over the tabernacle of the testimony, and over all its furnishings</u>, . . . And <u>the Levites shall keep guard over the tabernacle of the testimony</u>. . . ."* **ESV**. The Levites were fit for battle, but their battle was to prepare men spiritually for war and to protect the Tabernacle and its furnishings. There is a similar exemption for ministers from military service in these days in which I am living, however, within the military there are chaplains.

There were <u>two censuses</u> recorded in the book of Numbers. The first one was taken in the <u>second year after leaving Egypt;</u> and the other is recorded in **Numbers 26**. It was taken after 38 years of wandering in the wilderness, when Israel was camped in Moab just opposite Jericho as they readied to enter the Promised Land.

The results of the census were:

- Ruben: 46,500
- Simeon: 59,300
- Gad: 45,650
- Judah: 74,600
- Issachar: 54,400
- Zebulun: 57,400
- Ephraim: 40,500
- Manasseh: 32,200
- Benjamin: 35,400
- Dan 62,700
- Asher: 41,500
- Naphtali: 53,400

<u>The grand total: 603,550 firstborn sons</u> that were 20 years old and older.

These 603,550 men of war that were 20 years of age and older would make up the fighting army of Israel. **Verse 4**.

Now with such a number of men 20 years and older being 603,550, it would suggest that there were something like 2 or 3 million of the Children of Israel who were in the camp.

One might say: How is that? The firstborn sons that were 20 years old and older had two parents; and if you add the parents 1,207,100 to <u>603,550</u> firstborn sons above 20, it would raise the total number of the Children of Israel to <u>1,800,650</u>; and it is safe to say that there were at least the same number of 603,550 <u>girls above the age of 20,</u> and that would add <u>603,550</u> give a total of <u>2,414,000</u>. There were certainly included among the people those who were younger than 20 years of age, both male and female, therefore add another <u>1,207,100</u> and the total would rise to a grand total of <u>3,621,100</u> people.

This caravan was a huge traveling city of people to care for; but it was no problem for God, because all things are possible with God. **Luke 1:37**.

May I encourage you in the struggles that you may encounter in life. Never worry, always trust God. In the struggles and difficulties of life, remember this statement that Pastor Michael Catt made: "Jesus is there with you in the storm, and he will remain with you all the way to the shore. And having reached the shore, He will continue with you to the conclusion of your journey on earth, and take you to the place that Jesus is preparing for you."

Jesus told His disciples: *"These things I have spoken to you that in Me you may have peace. In the world you will have tribulation; but be of good cheer, I have overcome the world."* **John 16:33 NKJV**.

Chapter 2

The Positioning of The Tribes

The results of the census were 603,550 men of fighting age, who were fit for battle. **Verse 46**.

It is amazing to me to see how God took care of this huge caravan of complaining people. They would need food, water, medical care, sanitation, and so much more. Yet throughout all the 40 years in the wilderness not one person died from lack of care. Death only came because of a lack of trust in God.

In Deuteronomy 29 we read where Moses pointed out to the people how God cared for them in their wandering. They had taken so much of the good hand of God for granted. Moses reminded the people that their shoes and clothing did not wear out but they lasted for 40 years! That is unbelievable! Wow, they did not wear out! *"For forty years I led you through the wilderness, yet your clothes and sandals did not wear out. You had no bread or wine or other strong drink, but He gave you food so you would know that He is the Lord your God."* **Deuteronomy 29:5 & 6 NLT**.

God took such good care of Israel and did so many miracles among them that they became hardened to the good hand of God. The Bible Commentator John Phillips noted: *"Sometimes we become glory hardened, we become so used to seeing miracles that we no longer see them."* I think this could have been a malady of the Children of Israel.

Having taken the census, God now gives a special placement for each tribe. Here in **Chapter 2** we see listed how these armies of clans, or tribes were positioned. God had prepared specific places that each tribe must occupy while they were encamped, or "took up camp."

I have prepared a diagram as to how the various tribes were positioned around the Tabernacle. With each special place of encampment, each tribe also had a special identifying standard or banner.

The banners or standards of each tribe were stationed before their area of encampment. The banners contained the tribe name, with the symbol of each tribe. Those banners and their identifying symbols were as follows:

Judah: A lion

Issachar: A donkey

Zebulun: A Ship

Reuben: A mandrake

Simeon: A sword and shield of war

Gad: Tents

Ephraim: A bull

Manasseh: A palm tree & unicorn

Benjamin: A wolf

Dan: A horse of war and judgment

Asher: A cup pitcher

Naphtali: A deer or stag

Levi: The Priestly Breastplate.

Positioning of Tribes around the Tabernacle

Manasseh, Ephraim, Benjamin

Gershonites

Gad	*West*	Naphtali
	Tabernacle	
Ruben	**Court Yard**	Dan
Kohathites	*South* *North*	**Merarites**
Simeon	*East*	Asher

Moses, Aaron, Priests

Issachar, Judah, Zebulun

God also gave a special place where the Tribe of Levi, as the priestly tribe and charged with the care of the Tabernacle, were to be stationed. They were to be <u>positioned as a buffer around the borders of the Tabernacle and between the people and the Tabernacle</u>. The four families of the tribe of Levi have various responsibilities and positions:

- The **Gershonites** at the west boundary of the Tabernacle.

- The families of **Moses and Aaron** at the east boundary and door of the Tabernacle.

- The **Kohathites** at the north side boundary of the Tabernacle.

- The **Merarites** at the south side boundary of the Tabernacle.

The tribes positioned on the **west side** which is the back side of the Tabernacle are: Manasseh, Ephraim and Benjamin.

The families positioned on the **east side**, which is the entrance of the Tabernacle are: The families of Moses and Aaron; the tribes of Issachar, Judah, and Zebulun.

The tribes positioned on the **north side** of the Tabernacle are: Gad, Ruben, and Simeon.

The tribes positioned on the **south side** of the Tabernacle are: Naphtali, Dan, and Asher.

I feel there is much to learn from how God has placed the various families around the Tabernacle. Families can benefit by staying informed with each other and understanding their mission in life. I feel that it is important and necessary for families to know their heritage and where their homeland is located. It is also important that families learn from both the successes and the failures of past family members; this will help to successfully pattern their life. It is important to learn from one's past in order to benefit in securing a good future.

The greatest benefit of the past is the work of Jesus Christ which secured for every believer a future home in heaven that will last throughout eternity. Jesus secured for all believers eternal life.

The sins of the past do not have to affect the future. Jesus died for the sins of the past, the sins of today, and the sins of the future. Because of the finished work of Jesus Christ, God the Father makes every believer a new creation, destroys their past failures, and is righteous and just to place them in the home that Jesus is now preparing for them. **2 Corinthians 5:17**.

The banner and standard of the believer is the love of God. Jesus told His disciples: *"By this all will know that you are My disciples, if you have love for one another."* **John 13:35 NKJV**.

As the old children's Gospel song goes: *"His Banner Over Me is Love."*

John the Beloved wrote: *"Beloved, let us love one another, for love is of God; and everyone who loves is born of God and knows God."* **1 John 4:7 NKJV**.

Chapter 3

The Levites

The responsibility of every tribe was to fight. The responsibility of the Levites was to protect and guard over the people and the Tabernacle: *"Bring the tribe of Levi near, and set them before Aaron the priest, that they may minister to him. They shall <u>keep guard over him and over the whole congregation</u> before the tent of meeting, as they minister at the tabernacle. They shall <u>guard all the furnishings of the tent of meeting,</u> and <u>keep guard over the people of Israel</u> as they minister at the tabernacle."* **Verses 5 – 8 ESV**.

The Levites were the priestly tribe and they belonged to the Lord and were charged with guarding the people, the Tabernacle, its furnishings and the spiritual welfare of the people. Nadab and Abihu had died for offering "strange fire" before the Lord, leaving Eleazar and Ithamar as the remaining sons of Aaron.

The Levites were to serve Aaron and his sons as assistants in worship, and they were also chosen by God as a substitute firstborn of all the families of Israel. **Verses 11 – 13:** *"And the Lord spoke to Moses, saying, "Behold, I have taken the Levites from among the people of Israel instead of every firstborn who opens the womb among the people of Israel. The Levites shall be mine, for all the firstborn are mine. On the day that I struck down all the firstborn in the land of Egypt, I consecrated for my own all the firstborn in Israel, both of man and of beast. They shall be mine: I am the Lord."* **ESV**

The tenth plague that God brought upon Egypt was the death of the firstborn. However, with the impending plague God had a special provision as a way of escape. The blood of the Passover Lamb was that escape. The blood meant that the firstborn and family inside belonged to the Lord. Any family that took the blood of the Passover Lamb and wiped that blood upon the lintel and door post was a sign to the death angel to pass over that house; the blood saved the life of the firstborn. That firstborn son belonged to the Lord. He was then dedicated to the Lord. Those children belonged to the Lord.

Here at Sinai, God now had Moses to take a special census of the Tribe of Levi. The results were: Moses, Aaron, and Aaron's two sons, Nadab, Abihu, Eleazar, and Ithamar were God's leaders, the High Priest and priests before the Lord. The tribe of Levi were to be the assistants of Aaron and his sons. Levi had three sons: Gershon, Kohath, and Merari.

Now God told Moses to take a census of all the firstborn males of the tribe of Levi that were one month old and older. The results of the census were:

- The number of firstborn males one month and older of the clan of Gershon was <u>7,500</u>.
- The number of firstborn males one month and older of the clan of Kohath was <u>8,600</u>.
- The number of the firstborn males one month and older of the clan of Eleazar was <u>6,200</u>.
- The grand total of the firstborn males one month and older of the Tribe of Levi was <u>22,000 people</u>.

The reason for taking a census of the Tribe of Levi was to get the number of firstborn males one month old and older. The reason for the "one month" was that at the time of the taking of this census, it had been one month since they left Egypt and a one month old child would have been born at the time of the Passover. That number was to be compared with the number of all the firstborn of all the other tribes of Israel that were one month old and older. *And the Lord said to Moses, "List all the firstborn males of the people of Israel, from a month old and upward, taking the number of their names. <u>And you shall take the Levites for me—I am the Lord—instead of all the firstborn among the people of Israel, and the cattle of the Levites instead of all the firstborn among the cattle of the people of Israel.</u>"* **Verses 40 – 41 ESV**.

The concluding number from the taking of the census was that there were 22,273 firstborn males among the children of Israel, and there were <u>22,000</u> firstborn males among the tribe of Levi. This left a 273 shortfall in the number of firstborn male Levite substitutes available to serve in the place of the number of firstborn males from all the people.

To solve this problem, God had Moses take a redemption price from all the people of Israel of five shekels of silver (about 2 ounces of silver) from each family as payment for the shortfall. The total of the silver tax came to 1,365 shekels of silver, perhaps weighing around 34 pounds of silver.

God is a God of unity and order, not of confusion and discord. Each clan of the Levites had a special place to encamp. They were especially appointed by God to guard the spiritual welfare of the people; and they also had special responsibilities in worship, which are listed here:

<u>Gershon</u> was responsible for the tent and the curtains. **Verses 21 – 26**.

<u>Kohath</u> was responsible for the inside curtain, the furnishings of the sanctuary, the ark, the table, the lampstand, the altars and vessels. **Verses 27 – 31**.

<u>Eleazar</u>, the son of Aaron, was the chief administrator and in charge of the general oversight of the Levites. **Verse 32**.

<u>Merari</u> was responsible for frames, bars, pillars, bases, and their accessories. **Verses 33 – 37**.

Did you know that God has a special responsibility for you? Yes, He does. Therefore, seek to discover that special mission and responsibility. That mission and responsibility will guard the lives of others.

Chapter 4

Priestly Duties

The census continues, and the duties of the various priestly families are given. An active priest served between the ages of <u>30 years old through 50 of age</u>. **Verse 3**.

At the <u>age of 25</u> a person could begin preparing for the priesthood; it was a period of apprenticeship. When the priest reached the <u>age of 50</u>, he was required to retire from the <u>heavy work</u> of worship.

The work in the Tabernacle was difficult work, and it required the priest to be a person of strength, in good health, and fit for the task. In **Numbers 8:23 – 26** we read: *"This is the rule the Levites must follow: They must begin serving in the Tabernacle at the age of twenty-five, and they must retire at the age of fifty. After retirement they may assist their fellow Levites by performing guard duty at the Tabernacle, but they may not officiate in the service. This is how you will assign duties to the Levites."* **NLT**.

When God calls one to a ministry, He leaves nothing undone. He leaves no area uncovered. God is our <u>guide</u>, our <u>supplier</u>, our <u>encourager</u>, our <u>refuge</u>, our <u>resource for refreshing</u>, our <u>source of knowledge</u>, our <u>instructor in wisdom</u>, our <u>strength for every task</u>, our <u>ever present help</u> in time of trouble, and so much more.

Here God gives instruction as to how each clan was to disassemble the Tabernacle in a holy way that would give God the glory and honor that He deserves. Everything was to be respectfully disassembled; and after the disassembly has been completed, Aaron and his sons would inspect everything and cover everything.

The <u>duties of the Kohathites</u> are listed in **Verses 4 – 20**. Their responsibility was for the furnishings and utensils inside the sanctuary of the Tabernacle, including both altars. It was the duty of Aaron and his sons to take down the inner curtain, fold it, and lay it across the Ark of the Covenant; and then they were to cover the curtain with fine goat skin leather, and cover the goat skin with a special dark blue cloth. After that, the poles were to be placed through the rings on the Ark of the Covenant. **Verses 5 & 6**.

The Table of Showbread was covered with a dark blue cloth, and then a scarlet cloth was placed over the dark blue cloth, and a fine badger skin was draped over the scarlet cloth. After this was completed, the poles were inserted through the rings of the Table of Showbread. **Verse 8**.

The Lampstand was cleaned and prepared for moving and then covered with a dark blue cloth and its utensils placed in a fine goatskin bundle and placed on the frame. **Verses 9 & 10**.

The Golden Altar was cleaned, the ashes discarded, and everything covered with a dark blue cloth, and upon that a layer of fine goat skin, and the poles inserted in the rings. **Verses 11 – 12**.

Eleazar, the son of Aaron, was responsible for the general supervision of the move as well as for the oil, incense, grain offering, and anointing oil. **Verse 16**.

To vary from this pattern and plan would result in death of the person who committed the offense. **Verses 17 – 21**.

The Gershonite family was responsible for the moving of all the prepared items of the Tabernacle, and Aaron's sons, Nadab, Abihu, Eleazar, and Ithamar, served as the superintendents in the move. **Verses 24 – 28**.

The Merarite family was also responsible for carrying the wall supports of the outer court in the move. **Verses 31 – 33**.

There was no demeaning task here. All things were of great importance. Never feel that the ministry of another person is greater than what God has given you. God takes special pleasure in your ministry, and He takes great pleasure in you; you are His special child. *"Each man was assigned his task and told what to carry, just as the Lord had commanded through Moses."* **Verse 49 NLT**.

The number taken in the census of each clan was as follows:

- The Kohathites: 2,750
- The Gershonites: 2,630
- The Merarites: 3,200
- The total number of men 30 years to 50 years old: 8,580.

All things were done in order and according to the plan of God. That is the way we must always do the calling that God has given to us: *"Let all things be done decently and in order."* *as* the Apostle Paul writes in **1 Corinthians 14:40 NKJV**.

Chapter 5

Restitution

There are three laws that are being addressed here: God's Law of Separation, God's Law of Recompense, and God's Law of Jealousy.

1. <u>The Law of Separation</u> had to do with the health of the people within the camp.
2. <u>The Law of Recompense</u> had to do with the those who have been injured in the camp by theft or deception.
3. <u>The Law of Jealousy</u> had to do with a wife who had been falsely accused of adultery by a jealous husband.

Each these laws have to do with restoring confidence, and bringing peace to the camp. God is the God of peace, love, unity, and trust; and God desires His people to live in peace and love, and He wants them to live their lives in a spirit of unity and trust.

What is being pointed out in each of these laws is: <u>God hates sin</u>, and <u>all sin is against God</u>. There are two words that are used in describing man's natural depravity and his unholy condition before God:

Sin: <u>Falling short</u> of the glory of God

Trespasses: <u>Crossing the line</u> of the expectations of God.

Jesus is the only remedy, the only cure for sin; and to receive that remedy and cure for sin one must confess his sins before God and make his decision known before man. The remedy for sin is freely given; but the remedy must be freely received by each individual person in order for it to be applied to his life.

Scripture tells us that God is not willing that anyone should perish; we know that God longs for each person to come to a point in his life where he repents of his sin by confessing his sin and asking forgiveness of his sin. **2 Peter 3:9**.

All people are born into a world of sin, and therefore everyone is born a sinner and lives his life in sin; but not everyone will confess his sins. That is sad, but it shows the power of the principalities and powers of this world and the workers of iniquity that are at work against God's Good News for them.

The first law covered is the <u>Law of Separation</u>. God gives His requirements for those who have contracted any contagious disease and what is required of a person who has contracted such a disease. The disease mentioned here is leprosy, but it could be any similar detestable disease. The law is for such a person to be quarantined to protect the people from contacting such a disease. **Verses 1 – 3**.

The Apostle Paul writes that the things that happened in the Old Testament were written as examples for us. **1 Corinthians 10:1 – 13**. Here in **Chapter 5** the leper is to be separated from others because of his disease. In the same way, sin separates mankind from God because of the incurable disease of sin. **Verses 1 – 4**.

The next law is the <u>Law of Recompense</u> for theft or fraud. The Apostle Paul writes that the things that happened in the Old Testament were written as examples for us. **1 Corinthians 10:1 – 13**.

Any sin that is committed against another person is also a betrayal and sin against the Lord. This sin was committed against another person by destroying some asset of the person, and destroying a proper relationship with God. This sin may have gone undiscovered, and the person whose property has been taken may have died, not realizing what has happened; if that is the case, then when the crime has been discovered, the next of kin is to receive the repayment from the one who has stolen it.

The judgment of God was that the offender must restore the full price of the asset plus an added 20% increase as payment. If the person in which the asset was taken was dead, then the nearest of kin was to receive the restitution payment. Any sin against others and God must be confessed openly before the congregation as well as to God Himself.

The sin addressed here is for things that have been stolen, or taken by fraud. God desires for these things to be resolved now and before the Children of Israel enter the Promised Land. God wanted to make sure that there was no cause for any squabble that might distract someone from giving his full attention to the possessing of the land, **Verses 5 – 10**. This situation is also covered in **Leviticus 6:1 – 5**.

The third law is God's <u>Law of Jealousy</u>. Upon the first reading of this chapter, it seems as though God was being hard on the wife who has been <u>accused of committing adultery</u>, or has been <u>falsely accused of committing adultery</u>, and requires nothing of the husband. But that is not the case here. Women of that day had little recourse when accused of adultery; and any accusation of unfaithfulness would destroy their reputation, or at least they would suffer from their reputation being marred and unredeemable.

Israel is often compared to an unfaithful wife to God in Scripture. Ezekiel gives such a comparison in **Ezekiel 16:15 – 43**. God says that He is a jealous God. What is meant by that? It means that God is righteous, true, holy and just; and in being so, He will not tolerate anything that is not holy, and set apart, to share in His holy presence. What do we know about God?

We know that "God is," He is holy, and He never changes, but man does. We know that God is eternal, and being eternal means that he always has been and will always be; it also means that everything that "is" has been created by Him. In His response to Moses as to what he should tell the Children of Israel who has sent him to them, God told Moses to say that His name is "I AM," **Exodus 3:14**. Jehovah God is ever-present, all things exist in His "<u>eternal</u> now" presence. Anything other than "The One God" is a "false god," and God will respond with holy anger and with His holy wrath to anything else, for He is a jealous God.

The jealousy that is addressed here is not a holy jealousy. It is a selfish jealousy and may have been unfounded. This jealousy is one that causes division, not unity. Remember when God created man and woman that He said: *"Therefore a man shall leave his father and mother and be joined to his wife, and they shall become one flesh."* **Genesis 2:24 NKJV**. Eve was to be a helpmeet, a helper that was comparable to Adam; and God said that the two were to become one.

Something has happened in this situation that has caused this godly unity to come into question, and it has brought about a mistrust. The mistrust has caused an unholy jealousy. Jealousy is anger; and the sun has gone down on this anger many times. This situation was "not" what God expected or desired of the husband and wife.

In this situation, God was the only One who knew the truth; therefore, God would be the only Judge in this situation, and not a man. The priest was not the judge. He was the one appointed by God to officiate the process of revealing the truth.

In Scripture God says that He is a jealous God; what is meant by that? It means that God is righteous, true, holy and just; and in being so, He will not tolerate anything that is not holy, and set apart, to share in His holy presence. "God is," that means that He always has been and will always be; it means that everything that "is" has been created by Him. His response to Moses as to what he should tell the Children of Israel who has sent him to them, that His name is "I AM," **Exodus 3:14**. Jehovah God is ever-present; all things exist in His "<u>eternal now</u>" presence. Anything other than "The One God" is a "false god," and God will respond with holy anger and with His holy wrath to anything else, for He is a jealous God.

This jealousy that is being dealt with here <u>is not a holy jealousy; it is a selfish and unfounded jealousy</u>. This jealousy is one that causes division, not unity.

Remember when God created man and woman that He said: *"Therefore a man shall leave his father and mother and be joined to his wife, and they shall become one flesh."* **Genesis 2:24 NKJV**. Eve was to be a helpmeet, a helper that was comparable to him; the two shall become one.

Now, women of that day had little or no recourse when accused by a man, and this was "not" what God expected or desired of a husband and wife.

God's process in bringing about the truth was grievous, and sin is grievous. There is great shame here for the woman to endure, but her only recourse is God. Notice what the woman is to say when the priest explains to the woman what must be done: *"Now may this water that brings the curse enter your body and cause your abdomen to swell and your womb to shrivel. And the woman will be required to say, 'Yes, let it be so.'"* **Verse 22 NLT**.

Remember, this sin has to do with the jealousy of the husband and the <u>defense of the wife</u> with the false accusation of adultery; <u>she has not been caught in the act of adultery</u>.

Again, the question is: Is the wife genuinely guilty, or has something happened to cause her husband to be jealous? The remedy is that God will be the judge. The problem with the husband is envy, distrust, unfaithfulness, jealousy, bitterness, anger, clamor and malice. Read **Ephesians 4:31 & 32**.

There is a lack of trust here; and it is of great importance for married partners to have trust in each other. There may have been some evil intent brought upon the husband by some person bent on causing discord.

A married couple is to be <u>bound together in love; the two must be one.</u> But something has happened here to bring about this jealousy.

The process here for the wife to endure is one that would cause great embarrassment, whether she was guilty or not. I would think that a wife who was guilty would not subject herself to such a gross and painful requirement.

The conclusion of this matter is:

<u>For the innocent wife</u>: *". . . if the woman has not defiled herself and is clean, then <u>she shall be free and shall conceive children</u>."* **Verse 28 ESV**.

I might point out that only God could restore such a marriage. And only a couple who have purposefully drawn near God could be restored. **James 4:7**.

<u>For the jealous husband</u>: *"The man shall be free from iniquity, but the woman shall bear her iniquity."* **Verse 31 ESV**. The husband here will have had his doubts either substantiated or refuted by God. If substantiated, the husband is not held to any guilt. But if the husband's feeling of jealousy is unsubstantiated and refuted by the judgment of God, he is guilty of unmitigated jealousy. The husband must make things right between himself and God, as well as himself and his innocent wife.

Chapter 6

The Nazirite Vow

Making vows before the Lord is a serious thing, and the Nazirite Vow stands out above all. The word of a person should be trusted; Jesus said that a believer should not swear at all. His said: *"But let your 'Yes' be 'Yes,' and your 'No,' No.'"* **Matthew 5:37 NKJV**. Don't be a person who is given to making vows, oaths, or swearing to affirm your word as true. Be known as a person of character and truth; be known as a person of your word, and let it be known to others that you are a person who is committed to obeying God.

Many times the reason for a person giving a vow is because his word cannot be trusted. We hear of believers who make special pledges to God for various reasons as a sense of proving their sincerity. A person who is "a man of his word" is not doubted and is without reason for his word to be substantiated.

I am sure you have heard people relay a situation in their lives where they were under great attack and they said to God: *"Lord, if You get me out of this situation, I will (fill in the bank)*. I would say that most people experience the dire situation being brought to a good conclusion, but they never do what they pledged to do.

The vow that is covered here is called "The Nazirite Vow." What is a Nazirite Vow? Nazirite means separated, dedicated, and given to God, and it could be taken by a man or a woman. The person who has taken The Nazirite Vow was considered to be the epitome of sanctification and being set apart to the Lord. Sometimes the Nazirite Vow was made for a lifetime, as in the case of Samuel being dedicated to God for life by his mother Hannah:

1 Samuel 1:11: *"Then she made a vow and said, 'O Lord of hosts, if You will indeed look on the affliction of your maidservant and remember me, and not forget your maidservant, but will give your maidservant a male child, then, <u>I will give him to the Lord all the days of his life, and no razor shall come upon his head</u>,"* **NKJV**.

Another example was proclaimed by The Angel of The Lord to the mother of Samson: **Judges 13:3 – 5:** *"And the Angel of the Lord appeared to the woman and said to her, 'Indeed now you are barren and have borne no children, but you shall conceive and bear a son. <u>Now therefore, please be careful not to drink wine or similar drink, and not to eat anything unclean. For behold, you shall conceive and bear a son. And no razor shall come upon his head, for the child shall be a Nazirite to God from the womb</u>; and he shall begin to deliver Israel out of the hand of the Philistines."* **NKJV**.

Also, we see where Zacharias, the father of John the Baptist, was told by the angel Gabriel in **Luke 1:8 – 17**: *". . . your wife Elizabeth will bear you a son, and you shall call his name John. . . . <u>He will also be filled with the Holy Spirit, even from his mother's womb</u>. And he will turn many of the children of Israel to the Lord their God. . . . "* **NKJV**.

The Apostle Paul took the Nazirite Vow at least two times to last for a limited period of time: **Acts 18:18** & **21:22 – 26**.

There are three requirements where special care must be taken in living out the Nazirite Vow. **Verses 3 - 21:**

1. Cannot have <u>anything to do with grapes</u>: juice, vinegar, wine, fresh, fermented, or dried. Why? Because grapes were considered a delicacy and a blessing.

2. <u>Cannot cut his hair</u> or adorn his hair in any way. The hair is considered a crown, and his head is to be dedicated to the Lord. *"The silver-haired head is <u>a crown</u> of glory, if it is found in the way of righteousness."* **Proverbs 16:31 NKJV**.

3. <u>He could not touch or come near any dead body</u>. Death comes upon all because of sin. The person who takes the Nazirite Vow cannot even touch the body of his parents when they die.

If the vow was broken for any reason, there was a Sin Offering, a Burnt Offering, a Peace offering, and a Grain Offering that must be made, **Verses 9 – 12**. And if the vow was taken for a special length of time, there were special sacrifices that were to be made: A Burnt Offering, a Sin Offering, a Grain Offering and a Peace Offering. **Verses 13 -20**.

The chapter ends with a blessing of the Children of Israel. This blessing by Aaron from God to be given to the Children of Israel is perhaps the most used and most desired blessing and benediction of all: *"The Lord bless you and keep you; the Lord make His face to shine upon you; the Lord lift up His countenance upon you and give you peace."* **Verses 24-26 ESV**.

I use this blessing and benediction in every wedding that I perform. This is the best thing that could be desired by any couple.

The truth of this blessing is as follows:

The source of all blessing is God. The Beatitudes of Jesus expound upon the great blessings from God.   God brings peace; He gives grace to receive, mercy to forgive, and love to share with others.

The Keeper of all believers is God. The 15th Century theologian Julian of Norwich wrote: *"There are three properties of every created being:*

1. *God made it,*
2. *God loves it,*
3. *God keeps it.*

God the Creator, the Lover, and the Keeper. Of this we need to understand that of all the things that have been made are already nothing when compared to the having and loving God, Who is unmade." **Julian of Norwich.**

- **The glory of the believer is God.**

- **The giver of grace to the believer is God.**

- **The holy presence of God is upon the believer.**

- **The giver of peace to the believer is God.**

In the presence of God there is peace, there is unity, there is blessing, and His glory is experienced. If you separate yourself to God, and commit yourself to God, He will bring great blessing to your soul.

Another like it is found in **Jude 24 & 25**: *"Now to Him who is able to keep you from stumbling, and to present your faultless before the presence of His glory with exceeding joy, to God our Savior, who alone is wise, be glory and majesty, dominion, and power, both now and forever, Amen."* **NKJV.**

Chapter 7

Offerings of Leaders

The longest chapter of the Pentateuch is **Numbers 7**. The Tabernacle has been finished, and it will now be consecrated to the Lord.   Every tribe is to give gifts and make offerings to the Lord. Each family of the tribe of Levi is also given what they need to carry out their special ministry.

The 11 tribes of the Children of Israel were to supply a total of <u>6 wagons and 12 oxen</u> to pull the wagons. It was <u>one wagon for every two leaders</u> of a tribe and <u>one ox for each tribe leader</u>. **Verses 2 – 6**. These were supplied to the three Levite clans to carry the furnishings and items of the Tabernacle:

- The clan of <u>Kohath</u> did <u>not receive any</u> because they were to carry the furnishings of the Tabernacle on their shoulders.

- The clan of <u>Gershon</u> was given two wagons and four oxen.

- The clan of <u>Merari</u> was given more: four wagons and eight oxen. The reason that they were given more was that they had more of the Tabernacle furnishings and items to carry.

One thing that is quickly noticed is that twelve times the same offerings were recorded word for word. *"... his offering was <u>one silver plate</u> whose weight was 130 shekels, <u>one silver basin</u> of 70 shekels, according to the shekel of the sanctuary,* *both of them full of fine flour mixed with oil for a grain offering; one golden dish of 10 shekels, full of incense; one bull from the herd, one ram, one male lamb a year old, for a burnt offering; one male goat for a sin offering; and for the sacrifice of peace offerings, two oxen, five rams, five male goats, and five male lambs a year old."* **Verses 13 – 17 ESV**.

Why didn't God have Moses say: *"And each tribe must give the same thing"?* It is because God loves His children and these things were personally written down in God's book. God takes the time to record all that every person does, whether good or bad. God desires to spend time with all His children. This is important to God. God is never in a hurry. He is purposeful and not bound by time. God is only bound by His own timing.

Each tribe gave their offering on a separate day:

1. The first day: The tribe of **Judah**.

2. The second day: The tribe of **Issachar**.

3. The third day: The tribe of **Zebulun**.

4. The fourth day: The tribe of **Reuben**.

5. The fifth day: The tribe of **Simeon**.

6. The sixth day: The tribe of **Gad**.

7. The seventh day: The tribe of **Ephraim**.

8. The eighth day: The tribe of **Manasseh**.

9. The ninth day: The tribe of **Benjamin**.

10. The tenth day: The tribe of **Dan**.

11. The eleventh day: The tribe of **Asher**.

12. The twelfth day: The tribe of **Naphtali**.

The offerings given by each tribe of the Children of Israel to the Tabernacle were as follows: **Verses 12 – 17; 18 – 23; 24 – 29, 30 – 35, 36 – 41, 42 – 47, 48 – 53, 54 – 59, 60 – 65, 66 – 71, 72 – 77, 78 – 83.**

- One silver platter that weighed 3¼ pounds and was filled with grain of the finest flour that had been mixed with oil.

- One silver basin that weighed 1¼ pounds and was filled with grain of the finest flour that had been mixed with oil.

- One golden container that weighed around four ounces which was filled with incense.

- A young bull, a ram, and a one-year-old male lamb to be used as a burnt offering.

- A male goat to be used as a sin offering.

- Two oxen, five rams, five male goats, and five one-year-old male lambs for a peace offering.

- The total weight of the 12 silver platters and 12 silver basins was 60 pounds. Each of the golden containers weighed 4 ounces, and the total weight of the 12 golden containers was 3 pounds. There was a total of 12 bulls, 12 rams, 12 one-year-old male lambs, 12 male goats, 24 young bulls, and 60 one-year-old male lambs.

The process of making all these first offerings was quite a job for Aaron, his sons, and the Levites. When God does something, it is always a glorious thing and it is done in a glorious way.

That thought should encourage every believer to always do all that he does for the Lord in a grand and glorious way that is well pleasing to God. Excellence is not an option in serving God; it is expected.

The Apostle Paul writes in **1 Corinthians 10:31**: *"Therefore, whether you eat or drink, or <u>whatever you do, do all to the glory of God</u>."* **NKJV**. Always give of your best to God.

Having finished receiving the gifts and offerings of the 12 tribes of Israel, Moses then goes into the newly constructed Tabernacle of worship. As he comes to the Ark of the Covenant, he hears the voice of God speaking to him about the Golden Lampstand and the Levites. God speaks to Him about the Golden Lampstand and the programed procedure in ordaining the final tribe of the Children of Israel. Now the tribe of Levi would have their special day of committing themselves to God as His priestly tribe. This would be their day of ordination to the ministry. **Verse 89**.

Chapter 8

Tabernacle Furniture

Chapter 8 begins with how the Golden Lampstand is to be arranged inside the Tabernacle, and the dedication ceremony of the Levites, their tenure of service as well as their retirement. Perhaps we could use the term the <u>ordination service</u> here. God desires and takes pleasure in His ministers being publicly dedicated, or ordained into service, and that believers should share in the celebration. Today we ordain ministers to the ministry.

The Golden Lampstand was made according to the exact pattern that God gave to Moses; and it was positioned exactly where God desired for it to be placed. It was placed against the south side wall of the Holy Place. **Exodus 25:31 – 40**.

There were no windows in the Tabernacle, and the only source of light was at the single entrance curtain of the Tabernacle which was at the east and the light that would come from the Golden Lampstand.

The significance of the Lampstand was all about God: God is the very source of light, Jesus is the Light of the world, and the lampstand represented the light of God. At creation, the first act of God was: *"Let there be light, and there was light."* **John 8:12; John 1:5 & Genesis 1:3 NKJV**. Where light is, darkness cannot be; and all believers are to be a light to the world. **Matthew 5:14 – 16**.

The Golden Lampstand had seven cups that were filled with oil and Aaron was responsible for keeping the cups filled with oil, lit, focused, and cleaned. God tells Moses that the cups of the Golden Lampstand were to be focused forward giving light to the north wall east and west borders of the Holy Place of the Tabernacle. The seven lamps were to light up the whole Holy Place, from the west of the Tabernacle in the direction of the Altar of Incense, and the center curtain, the Table of Showbread, and to the east in the direction of the curtain of entrance of the Tabernacle.

Now comes the ordination or dedication service for the Levites. The Levites were chosen by God to be His priestly tribe; and they were to serve as the substitute for all the firstborn of Israel, who were saved from death by the blood of the Passover lamb at the original Passover in Egypt. God had said that all the firstborn belonged to Him. **Exodus 13:2:** *"Consecrate to Me all the firstborn, . . . it is Mine."* **NKJV**.

The Levites were a chosen people, and as a chosen people, they were to be a holy people. This dedication service for the Levites was to be the official and public inaugural launching of their service to God as His ministers.

First of all, <u>they were to be cleansed</u>, thoroughly washed and sprinkled with a water that had been mixed with the ashes from the Altar of Burnt Offering of a red heifer. We read of this purification water in **Numbers 19:9**: *"Then a man <u>who is clean shall gather up the ashes of the heifer</u>, and store them outside the camp in a clean place; and they shall be kept for the congregation of the children of Israel <u>for the water of purification; it is for purifying from sin</u>."* **NKJV**.

Everything is to be cleaned. The Levites were to shave all the hair from their body so that the holy water would not be polluted as it was poured upon their body. **Verse 6**.

After the Levites had been cleaned and sprinkled with the holy water upon their shaved body, <u>Aaron would offer a Sin Offering, a Burnt Offering, and give a wave offering</u> from the children of Israel, of whom the tribe of Levites had been selected as the substitute for the firstborn. These offerings were followed by the people standing before the Levites with their hands upon them in a <u>symbolic wave offering</u>. **Verses 8 – 13**.

The conclusion of this ceremony would officially declare the Levites to be <u>the atonement for the firstborn</u> and God's servants. **Verses 17 & 18**: *"For all the firstborn among the people of Israel are mine, both of man and of beast. On the day that I struck down all the firstborn in the land of Egypt <u>I consecrated them for myself, and I have taken the Levites instead of all the firstborn among the people of Israel</u>."* **ESV**.

The Levites would not only be a substitute for all the firstborn, but they were also given as a gift from God to Aaron and his sons to be their assistants in worship. **Verse 19**.

God concludes by giving the tenure for the Levites who serve in the Tabernacle for Worship. The length of time was from the ages of 25 – 50. Five years were for training, or a time of apprenticeship; and the actual length of service in the Tabernacle was from 30 years old to 50 years of age. **Verses 24 – 36**: *"This applies to the Levites: from twenty-five years old and upward they shall come to do duty in the service of the tent of meeting. <u>And from the age of fifty years they shall withdraw from the duty of the service and serve no more.</u> They minister to their brothers in the tent of meeting by keeping guard, but they shall do no service. Thus shall you do to the Levites in assigning their duties."* **ESV**.

The Levites were not their own; they did not do their ministry as *they* felt was right. They belonged to God and they must serve exactly as God gave them commands.

Now, God did not say that the Levite priests were not to do any service at all after they retired. God said that they were not to do the "difficult work" after they reached the age of 50.

The only time that any believer retires from all service is when God takes him to be with Him in heaven. At that time God will say as the master said in the parable of the talents: ". . . *'Well done, good and faithful servant; you have been faithful over a few things, I will make you ruler over many things. Enter into the joy of your lord.'* " **Matthew 25:23 NKJV**.

The believer is to be faithful in all things that God has given him to do. At the Judgment Seat of Christ, or the Bema, all believers will be judged for the things that they have done for God, whether good or bad; we read in **2 Corinthians 5:9 - 11:** "*. . . make it our aim, whether present or absent, to be well pleasing to Him. For we must all appear before the judgment seat of Christ, that each one may receive the things done in the body, according to what he has done, whether good or bad. . ."* **NKJV**.

Though believers will not experience the wrath of God, they will suffer the judgment of God where crowns will be taken away. Although believers will not experience rejection by God to everlasting punishment, they will publicly experience the disappointment of God. That is a fearful thing, and it should spur the believer on to being a faithful servant.

John the Beloved writes in the Book of Revelation: *"Blessed and holy is he who has part in <u>the first resurrection</u>. Over such the second death has no power, but <u>they shall be priests of God and of Christ, and shall reign with Him a thousand years</u>."* **Revelation 20:6 NKJV**, and *"Then I saw a great white throne and Him who sat on it, . . . And the dead were judged according to their works, by the things which were written in the books. . . . This is the second death. And anyone not found written in the Book of Life was cast into the lake of fire."* **20:11 – 15 NKJV**

What I'm saying is that believers do not "retire;" they are "re-tired." They just have a new set of tires put on them to complete their ministry.

As one gets older, he can no longer do the stressful and heavy things that he used to do; but he has much knowledge, great understanding, and useful wisdom from which those younger than he can benefit.

"After retirement they may assist their fellow Levites by performing guard duty at the Tabernacle, but they may not officiate in the service. This is how you will assign duties to the Levites." **Verse 26 NLT**.

Chapter 9

The Second Passover

The children of Israel are still at Sinai, they have been there for two years and God has not moved them. Some of the children of Israel may have felt that they had been there too long; but the reason God has not had them to continue on their journey to the Promised Land is that He is preparing them to lead a holy life, preparing them for holy worship, preparing His holy Tabernacle, preparing His worship leaders and priest, and preparing them to be a holy nation through whom He would send His Holy Son to be The Holy Lamb of God.

During these two years of encampment at Sinai, God has revealed to them His demands, His commands, and is preparing them, as well as training the spiritual leaders to lead in worship and in obedience to God's demands and commands. They will become the example for all believers as to how God works. **1 Corinthians 10:11:** *"Now all these things happened to them as examples, and they were written for our admonition, upon whom the ends of the ages have come."* **NKJV**.

During these two years God has given His chosen people His laws, His designed place of worship, He has called and dedicated His chosen leaders for worship, and now He will remind them that they need not only worship Him with a pure heart, but they must follow Him with a pure trust.

Remember, God is not bound by time; He is only bound to His perfect timing. God never gets into a hurry. God acts according to His holy word and divine will. **Isaiah 55:11**

In **Verse 1** we read that it is now the first month of the second year since they left Egypt, and they will soon celebrate the second Passover.

God has set the specific time for Passover; it would be observed on the 14th day of the first month at the going down of the sun. **Verses 2 – 5:** *"Let the people of Israel keep the Passover at its appointed time. On the fourteenth day of this month, at twilight, you shall keep it at its appointed time; according to all its statutes and all its rules you shall keep it." So Moses told the people of Israel that they should keep the Passover. And they kept the Passover in the first month, on the fourteenth day of the month, at twilight, in the wilderness of Sinai; according to all that the Lord commanded Moses, so the people of Israel did."* **ESV**

Passover was not a "one-time" event; it is to be celebrated by the children of Israel as an everlasting ordinance. **Exodus 13:10:** *"You shall therefore keep this ordinance in its season from year to year."* **NKJV**.

Jesus Christ, The Only Begotten Son of God, is the final Passover Lamb, and because of His blood that He willingly shed, everyone who accepts His sacrifice for their sins will be given eternal life. They will live forever in the place that He is preparing for them right now. That blood was holy, pure and powerful enough to cover the sins of the world; but just as at the first Passover in Egypt, the blood of the sacrificed Passover Lamb must be applied to the symbolic door of each person's life. If the blood has not been personally applied, that person will suffer the eternal death sentence that has been declared by God.

At this Passover, there were some men who desired to keep the Passover, but they had been ceremonially defiled because of touching a dead body. Perhaps a relative or close friend had just died; the actual reason is not made known. The disappointment that these men felt might be compared to someone not being allowed to celebrate Christmas or Easter.

Moses did not know what to do, so He asked God what should be done. **Verse 8**. In **James 1:5 – 8**, believers are told that in times of indecision and confusion they can ask God for wisdom in knowing what to do. A believer should not question if God would give him guidance because God has promised to give guidance to any believer who would ask for it; and He does not show favoritism. The believer is told to totally trust God; and having come to God, he is to do that thing that God puts in his mind, without doubting. It is a sure thing.

Moses asks God, and God answers. **Verse 10**: *"The Lord spoke to Moses, saying, ". . . If any one of you or of your descendants is unclean through touching a dead body, or is on a long journey, <u>he shall still keep the Passover to the Lord</u>."* **ESV**.

In worship, a person is to be ceremonially clean in order to participate in worship. Why is there an exception here? Because God is life, and the Passover was the celebration of life over death. The blood of the Lamb makes the difference by atoning for and conquering death.

There is no one who is refused access to the Blood of Jesus. *"For God so loved the world that He gave His only begotten Son, that <u>whoever believes in Him should not perish but have everlasting life</u>."* **John 3:16 NKJV**.

The sacrifice of Jesus is all inclusive, but it is exclusive to those who would not receive His sacrifice. The exclusion is made with a personal choice of rejecting God's Passover Lamb, Jesus Christ. God has not excluded you; you have excluded God.

God told Moses that those who are humanly clean, but choose not to be part of the Passover, are to be cut off from the people. This refusal to participate was not coerced; it was a personal choice. *"But if anyone who is clean and is not on a* journey <u>fails to keep the Passover, that person shall be cut off from his people because he did not bring the Lord's offering at its appointed time; that man shall bear his sin.</u>" **Verse 13 ESV**.

A truth that is seen here is that a person who may have gone through the "ceremonial cleansing or washing" does not make that person clean. Ceremonial laws only express what is required for a person to stand before a holy God. It is not possible for anyone to make himself clean; only the cleansing blood of Jesus will make one clean.   As the old hymn goes:

Whiter Than Snow

"Lord Jesus I long to be perfectly whole;

I want You forever to live in my soul,

Break down every idol; cast out every foe,

Now wash me and I shall be whiter than snow.

Whiter than snow, yes whiter than snow;

Now wash me and I shall be whiter than snow.

Lord Jesus for this I most humbly entreat,

I wait, blessed Lord, at Your crucified feet.

By faith, for my cleansing I see Your blood flow -

Now wash me and I shall be whiter than snow."

James Nicholson 1828 – 1876

The law is not wrong, and Jesus did not come to destroy the Law; He came to make it more clearly understood. **Matthew**

5:17: *"Do not think that I came to destroy the Law or the Prophets. I did not come to destroy but to fulfill."* **NKJV**.

Jesus has made the believer perfect before the Father. **2 Corinthians 5:21**. Jesus has made all believers ceremonially clean, and He wants all believers to come boldly before Him in worship and fellowship. **Hebrews 4:14 – 16**: *"Seeing then that we have a great High Priest who has passed through the heavens, Jesus the Son of God, let us hold fast our confession. For we do not have a High Priest who cannot sympathize with our weaknesses, but was in all points tempted as we are, yet without sin. Let us therefore come boldly to the throne of grace, that we may obtain mercy and find grace to help in time of need."* **NKJV**.

Next, we have the guidance of the Holy Spirit of God addressed. The symbol of God is the cloud by day and pillar of fire by night. The Latin term, "Coram Deo," *the presence of God,* can be applied here. It could also be called "The Shekinah Glory" of God; His glory is His presence.

The guidance system of God is how the cloud or pillar is positioned upon the Tabernacle. The Tabernacle is the tent of meeting with God. If the cloud or pillar covered the Tabernacle, the people were to stay encamped where they were. If the cloud was positioned above the Tabernacle, it was time to move and the people were to make ready to move. With that signal from God, the Tabernacle was to be disassembled and prepared to transport to the next place that God would lead them. **Verses 15 – 23**: *"On the day that the tabernacle was set up, the cloud covered the tabernacle, . . . at evening it was over the tabernacle like the appearance of fire until morning. . . And whenever the cloud lifted from over the tent, after that the people of Israel set out, and in the place where the cloud settled down, there the people of Israel camped. . . . As long as the cloud rested over the tabernacle, they remained in camp. Even when the cloud continued over the tabernacle many days, the people of Israel kept the charge of the Lord and did not set out. Sometimes the cloud was a few days* *over the tabernacle, . . . sometimes the cloud remained from evening until morning. . . . Whether it was two days, or a month, or a longer time, that the cloud continued over the tabernacle, ... They kept the charge of the Lord, at the command of the Lord by Moses."* **ESV**.

God still leads all believers and gives direction in their lives. The presence of God is with us for He is Emmanuel, God with us. He will never leave us nor forsake us. He can be trusted. So follow Him!

The hymn writer Joseph Gilmore wrote the lyrics to the hymn, "He Leadeth Me:"

<u>He Leadeth Me</u>

He leadeth me! O blessed thought!

O words with heavenly comfort fraught!

What-e'er I do, where-e'er I be,

Still 'tis God's hand that leadeth me.

He leadeth me, He leadeth me,

By His own hand He leadeth me:

His faithful follower I would be,

For by His hand He leadeth Me.

Joseph Gilmore 1834 – 1918

Chapter 10

Leaving Sinai

As the children of Israel prepare to move, they use the instructions that God has given them concerning following Him and obeying His exact instructions for travel.

It is a month after the celebration of the Second Passover and now the cloud rises and God tells Moses: "Head 'em up; Move 'em out! Let's go!"

God has given Moses instructions for a special pair of silver trumpets what would be used as a signal for the people. These were not silver representations of the ram's horn, shofar. The silver trumpets were the design of God.

The Hebrew historian Josephus, writes of them in his _Antiquities_ 3.291, as well as Louis H. Feldman in his _Studies in Hellenistic Judaism_, 1991.

God tells Moses to blow the trumpets to sound the alarm with the appropriate signal relating to the occasion. If one trumpet is blown, then all the people are to come to the Tabernacle; if two trumpets are blown together, only the heads of each tribe are to come to the Tabernacle. At the "advance the camp sound" everyone was to prepare for travel. **Verses 2 – 10**.

The first move was from Sinai to Paran. There is an order in the moving procedure. **11 - 36**:

- Judah was to be in the lead with their banner before them. **Verse 14**

- Issachar with their banner before them. **Verse 15**

- Zebulun with their banner before them. **Verse 16**

- The sons of Gershon and the sons of Merari with the disassembled Tabernacle. **Verse 17**

- Reuben with their banner before them. **Verse 18**

- Simeon with their banner before them. **Verse 19**

- Gad with their banner before them. **Verse 20**

- The Kohathites with the holy furniture of the Tabernacle. **Verse 21**

- Ephraim with their banner before them. **Verse 22**

- Manasseh with their banner before them. **Verse 23**

- Benjamin with their banner before them. **Verse 24**

- Dan with their banner before them; they were the protection of the people from attack at the rear. **Verse 25**

- Asher with their banner before them. **Verse 26**

We read here that Moses talked with his brother-in-law Hobab about the joy of entering the Promised Land. But Hobab, the son of Reuel the Midianite priest, (Reuel was also called Jethro, **Exodus 18**) was the brother of Moses' wife

Zipporah. He felt that he should return to his home in Midian since the children of Israel were about to continue their journey to Canaan. **Exodus 2:22 & 3:1**. Zipporah was the mother of Moses' two sons: Gershom and Eliezer. **Exodus 2:22**.

Moses was disappointed to hear this news, and he did not want Hobab to leave. Moses was able to convince him to remain with them as they traveled. **Verses 29 – 32**: *And Moses said to Hobab the son of Reuel the Midianite, Moses' father-in-law, "We are setting out for the place of which the Lord said, 'I will give it to you.' <u>Come with us, and we will do good to you, for the Lord has promised good to Israel</u>." But he said to him, "<u>I will not go. I will depart to my own land and to my kindred</u>." And he said, "<u>Please do not leave us, for you know where we should camp in the wilderness, and you will serve as eyes for us. And if you do go with us, whatever good the Lord will do to us, the same will we do to you</u>."* **ESV**.

Sometimes people need to be assured of your love for them. Believers should always be sensitive to the feelings of others. We read in **Chapter 12** that Moses was such a person: *"Now the man Moses was very humble, more than all men who were on the face of the earth."* **Numbers 12:3 NKJV**.

When everyone and everything was ready and in place as the Lord had commanded, the journey to the Promised Land resumed. Moses was about 82 years of age now.

The Ark of the Covenant, that was carried upon the shoulders of the Kohathites, in concert with the cloud and pillar, was the symbolic focus of the leadership of God as the children of Israel traveled; and as they set out, the call of Moses was: *"Rise up, O Lord! Let Your enemies be scattered, let those who hate You flee before you."* And when it rested, he said: *"Return, O Lord, to the many thousands of Israel."* Moses was saying: God be with us as we travel, protect us, and keep us in Your care. When time came to set up camp, Moses prayed:

Stay with us O God; may Your holy presence always be with us.

This is similar to a prayer that we might pray as we begin a journey or as we lie down at night and rise with the dawn of each new day. We ask God to be with us, protect us, care for us, and lead us.

Chapter 11

Rebellion

The children of Israel were very good at complaining; they always found a reason to murmur. If you were to look up the word murmur, it would have a picture of the children of Israel posted next to the definition.

They could not be satisfied. They were always finding things to complain about. Do you know people like that? I know many of them. They are easy to find and are in great supply.

Solomon writes that God does not overlook complaining! One of the things that God hates is the person who causes discord among the brethren. **Proverbs 6:16 – 19**.

These people openly and together expressed their displeasure with the leadership of God. God in turn openly and mightily unleashes His fire of destruction upon these dissenters and rebels.

What were they complaining about? They are complaining about God's blessing upon them. They do not like what God has given them to eat. They were saying, *"It's not fair!"* They are saying that they want something else other than this heavenly food, this manna that God provided every morning. Well, that is exactly what God would now do; He would be fair and just with them, and not merciful and gracious.

To be fair is to act with righteous justice for what a person does; to be merciful is not to be fair. To be <u>merciful is not to</u>

give a person "what he deserves," and to be gracious is not to be fair and just and give to someone "what they do not deserve."

Here, God is righteous, just and fair, giving these dissenters and rebels what they deserve. Perhaps as they were actively engaged in their murmuring, God suddenly unleashes holy fire and judgment upon the dissenters and rebels, as we read in **Verse 1**.

Now the complaining changed into pleading with Moses to ask God for mercy; they pleaded for the judgment of God's fire to end. And God answered the intercessory prayer of Moses for the repentant people. **Verses 2 & 3**.

The complaining will quickly rekindle as they continue to complain about what they have to eat. This world is full of protestors, anarchists, and rebels. The confusing thing is that these types of people easily find a huge following. Though it should be obvious that they are wrong, they are seen to be right and just. Even good people are easily taken in by them.

Who was it that started and flamed this fire of discontent? It was the *"mixed multitude who were among them."* **Verse 4**. Now be careful in life to whom you lean your ear. Do not give unbelievers or people with a rebellious spirit any credibility. When you hear something that leads to dissent, question it. If you are uncertain, go to God for the answer. When rebellious and unbelieving people use Scripture, read that Scripture for yourself and ask the Holy Spirit for understanding. As you begin to study Scripture, the Holy Spirit will lead you to other verses in Scripture until you have a clear understanding.

Remember that when the Holy Spirit led Jesus into the wilderness to be tempted by Satan, Satan quoted Scripture to Jesus, but he misused it. Never give way to the wiles and schemes of the devil. This is what happened to the children of

Israel. Satan knew what their besetting sin was and he took advantage of it.

This continual complaining by the people began to take its toll on Moses, and he began to feel taken advantage of by God: *Moses said to the Lord, "Why have you dealt ill with your servant? And why have I not found favor in your sight, that you lay the burden of all this people on me?"* **Verse 11 ESV**.

Being around complaining people will discourage the greatest of men. Moses finally asks God to just take his life and relieve him of this calling. **Verse 15**.

God's response to Moses was to get the 70 elders and then He Himself would talk with them and they would share in the burden with Moses. **Verses 16 & 17**.

The message that God gave to the 70 and Moses was not a good one; yes, they would have meat, but with the meat that they requested would come a devastating plague. **Verses 18 – 20**.

Moses did not understand. He thought that God was asking him to provide meat for these 2 to 3 million people for a month. **Verse 22**: *"Shall flocks and herds be slaughtered for them, and be enough for them? Or shall all the fish of the sea be gathered together for them, and be enough for them?"* **ESV**

Here is the truth: Never question God; just obey God. We do not need to know how or why; we only need to know Who and when. When God says now, He means now.

There was a one-time thing that happened here, and that was that the Spirit of God came upon the 70 and they began to proclaim the word of the Lord to the people. *". . . and it happened, when the Spirit rested upon them, that they prophesied, <u>though they never did so again</u>."* **Verse 25 NKJV.**

Now there were two men, Eldad and Medad, who were among the 70 but who were not present at the meeting at the

Tabernacle with the others, and having heard about what God had said to those at the Tabernacle, they began to proclaim the news, as though they had been with the group at the Tabernacle. They preached the message in the camp as though they had been with the main group. Joshua heard about this and complained to Moses. His reasoning was that he thought these two men might contend with the authority of Moses. However, Moses was not concerned at all about the two men because they were proclaiming the correct message to the people.

The Apostle Paul writes of something similar in **Philippians 1:15 – 18**: *"Some indeed preach Christ even from envy and strife, and some also from goodwill: The former preach Christ from selfish ambition, not sincerely, supposing to add affliction to my chains; but the latter out of love, knowing that I am appointed for the defense of the gospel. What then? Only that in every way, whether in pretense or in truth, Christ is preached; and in this I rejoice, yes, and will rejoice."* **NKJV**.

Spend your time being faithful in what God has called you to do and allow God to take care of what is done for wrong reasons.

Now this was a huge amount of quail: There were quail throughout the camp about <u>18" high for about a mile around the camp</u>, **Verse 31**. The people gathered about <u>3 to 6 bushels</u> of quail. **Verse 32**. Can you imagine the noise that their wings made?

I remember as a boy when my grandpa Thomas had a "chicken catching." He raised chickens for a poultry company in a huge chicken house. The chicken company delivered the biddy chickens, and my Papaw and Mamaw Thomas would raise them in that huge chicken house until the chickens reached the desired age and size.

When the time came to gather the chickens, people from all around the area would come to help catch the chickens and put them into cages and then stack the cages upon this large semi-truck bed. My Mamaw would cook a big feast for all the hands. It was a grand time.

The chicken catching team was organized into:

- <u>Corallers</u>: Those who would herd the chickens and keep them together;
- <u>Catchers</u>: Those who caught the chicken by one leg and in bundles of three;
- <u>Carriers</u>: The children and young people who would hold three chickens by one leg each, and three in each hand;
- <u>Boxers</u>: Those who would receive the chickens to be pushed unceremoniously into a crate that was then place in rows upon the truck bed.

I remember the noise, the smell, and the dust. It made quite an impression upon me. Well, this catching in the wilderness was much more dramatic, and the people caught the quail all day, all throughout the night, and all the next day! **Verse 32.**

The fair and righteous judgment of God for the complaining of the people was a plague; and it was unexpected in its arrival and unyielding in its intensity. *"While the meat was yet between their teeth, before it was consumed, the anger of the Lord was kindled against the people, and the Lord struck down the people with a very great plague."* **Verse 33 ESV**.

The people did not have enough time to swallow the meat before God began the great plague among the gluttonous people.

The name that was given to the place of this plague was called: Kibroth Hattaavah, which means the graves of craving. Not only did they have to bury the people, but they had to bury, or burn, all the quail that they had craved. Be sure your sins will find you out. **Numbers 32:23**.

The desires of all believers should be to do the will of God and not to crave the pleasures of the world. What the world offers will not last; what God gives will endure throughout all eternity.

What was the root of this craving? It was enflamed by the "mixed multitude" that was among them. In every band of believers there are those who have mixed feelings; they mix the pleasures of the world with the promises of God. This is just like oil and water; they do not mix.

Stand upon God's promises and shun the fleeting pleasures of this world.

Chapter 12

Aaron and Miriam

In this chapter we see contempt and jealousy for fellow believers and leaders. Moses is the younger brother of Aaron and Miriam. Just as the brothers of Jesus had contempt for Him as they were growing up, so too did Aaron and Miriam.

Jesus's brothers and sisters questioned Jesus, as we read in **John 7:5:** *"For even His brothers did not believe in Him."* **NKJV.** Miriam and Aaron felt that they were equal in authority with Moses. *"And they said, "Has the Lord indeed spoken only through Moses? Has he not spoken through us also?"* **Verse 2**.

We read that the problem here was that Aaron and Miriam did not like the Ethiopian wife that Moses had taken. **Verse 1.** Who was this Ethiopian wife of Moses? We know that the wife of Moses was Zipporah, and she was the daughter of Jethro or Reuel who was a Midianite. We know that Zipporah and Moses had at least two children, two of them were boys who were named Gershom and Eliezer. **Exodus 2:22.**

But all we know here is that Aaron and Miriam did not like Moses' Ethiopian wife and that is all. Perhaps this Ethiopian woman had been part of the mixed multitude that came with Israel and at some time during the journey Moses married her. The marriage could have happened at this very moment, and the marriage caused a family disagreement. We have no real conclusive and reliable answer. Everything is left to mere speculation and opinion. Speculation is a guess and a guess cannot be trusted; one guess is as good as another. So, being speculation, the answer is not important. The important thing here is that Aaron and Miriam did not like the Ethiopian woman, and their dislike of her had no merit. We do know that she was un-named and the second wife of Moses. We also know that Aaron and Miriam were wrong, and they just needed to keep their opinion to themselves and be quiet.

Note that Moses is called very meek and humble. That does not mean that he was weak; it means that he desired to be pleasing. Moses would go to extremes to make people happy, but he was also able to unleash wrath when his humble measures failed. Jesus said that "the meek shall inherit the earth" in **Matthew 5:5**. Though meek, Moses was not listening to the opinion of Aaron and Miriam.

The real problem is found in **Verse 2**: *"They said, 'Has the Lord spoken only through Moses? Hasn't he spoken through us, too?" But the Lord heard them."* **NLT**.

Now at the burning bush Moses used his poor speaking ability as a reason not to go back to Egypt as the deliverer of the children of Israel. He complained to God that he was not a good speaker, and God told Moses that He would use Aaron as a spokesperson for Moses. **Exodus 4:13 & 14**: *"But Moses again pleaded, 'Lord, please! Send anyone else.' Then the Lord became angry with Moses. 'All right,' He said, 'What about your brother Aaron, the Levite? He is a good speaker. And look! He is on his way to meet you now..."* **NLT**.

Aaron and Miriam still considered themselves as co-leaders; but they were not. There cannot be two leaders. There must only be one leader and all others are followers or helpers.

Jesus said: *"No one can serve two masters; for either he will hate the one and love the other, or else he will be loyal to the one and despise the other. You cannot serve God and mammon."* **Matthew 6:24 NKJV**.

The Apostle Paul writes of leadership in **1 Corinthians 12:12 - 27**; he uses as an example the many parts of the body but one head. And in **Ephesians 5:22 – 33** Paul notes the leadership of the family. God is the head of the Trinity. Christ is the head of the church; and the husband is the head of the family. This is God's pattern of leadership. There can only be one leader.

God tells Aaron and Miriam that it is true that they are a prophet and a prophetess and that He does speak to them in dreams and visions; but He speaks to Moses face to face and with clear understanding as one friend to another. **Verses 6 – 9**.

 God is greatly angered at Aaron and Miriam and in His anger He strikes Miriam with full blown leprosy. **Verses 9 & 10**. Aaron quickly repents of his sins and pleads with Moses to speak to God, asking for forgiveness. **Verses 11 & 12**.

The decision of God was that He would forgive, but Miriam would have to be quarantined outside the camp for 7 days. Seven is the number of perfection and completion; it is also the number of God.

After the completion of her 7 days of quarantine, Miriam was healed of her leprosy and was taken back into the camp. **Verses 15 & 16**: *"So Miriam was shut outside the camp seven days, and the people did not set out on the march till Miriam was brought in again. After that, the people set out from Hazeroth, and camped in the wilderness of Paran."* **ESV**

Chapter 13

The Twelve Spies Sent Out

The children of Israel have arrived at Paran, and God has Moses to send out a team of explorers into the Promised Land. This fact finding team would spend 40 days exploring the land. At the beginning of this 40-day expedition by the 12 men to explore the Promised Land, there was great joy; but that great joy would quickly wane into great terror and ever increasing feelings of uncertainty by 10 of the 12 men by the time they returned with their report. The reason for the change in attitude by the 10 men was that they did not focus on the invisible power of God who was for them, but instead they focused upon the visible power of the opposition that was against them. They noted that it would take great risk to secure this "Land of Milk and Honey" that God had been telling them about.

Did you know that all winners take calculated risks? Those who cower to the threat against them will all lose. They are slaves to the situation and circumstances that prowl about them. These people live out their lives far short of what could have been had they taken the risk. The "easy way out" will keep you from the blessings of life. Risk takers are leaders, and they make positive differences in those who are around them.

In the life of the believer we call this risk-taking *faith*. Faith is based upon someone who is stronger that we are; faith is trust, and trust is hope. God is the source of our hope, He is our only reason for trust, and He is our sure defense and help in time of danger. **Psalm 46**: *"God is our refuge and strength, a very present help in trouble."* **Verse 1 NKJV**. *"But the Lord takes pleasure in those who fear him, in those who hope in his steadfast love."* **Psalm 147:11 ESV**; *"This hope we have as an anchor of the soul, both sure and steadfast, and which enters the Presence behind the veil,"* **Hebrews 6:19 NKJV**.

Who were these 12 tribal heads?

1. Shammua of Reuben, **Verse 4**
2. Shaphat of Simeon, **Verse 5**
3. Caleb of Judah, **Verse 6**
4. Igal of Issachar, **Verse 7**
5. Hoshea, later renamed Joshua by Moses, of Ephraim, **Verse 8**
6. Palti of Benjamin, **Verse 9**
7. Gaddiel of Zebulun, **Verse 10**
8. Gaddi of Manasseh, **Verse 11**
9. Ammiel of Dan, **Verse 12**
10. Sethur of Asher, **Verse 13**
11. Nahbi of Naphtali, **Verse 14**
12. Geuel of Gad, **Verse 15**.

Moses changes Hoshea's name to Joshua. Hoshea means *Salvation*; Joshua means *The Lord is salvation*.

For 40 days the 12 men explore this promised land, and after 40 days they return with their report. They all say that they indeed found the land flowing with great produce. They take note that just one cluster of grapes was so large that it took two men to carry the cluster back to the camp. **Verse 23**. They all agreed that the land was magnificent, and they had the proof with them. **Verse 27**.

Having presented this part of the report, the agreement ended. There was a problem: In order to take possession of this fruitful and prosperous land, they must overcome a very fearful, large, and powerful people. Many of the people of the land were much larger than they were; they seemed to be the size of a grasshoppers compared to these giants. They were the descendants of Anak. Anak was the father of a well-known clan of giant people.

And to make matters even worse, the land was entrenched with the vicious people of the Amalekites, Hittites, Jebusites, Amorites, and Canaanites. They were of the opinion that there was just too much risk involved in conquering the land.

The 10 spies saw the people but they did not consider the determining factor of God. God had said that He would be with them, and they refused to consider Him. These 10 men just kept up with their discouraging report.

Chapter 14

The Wrong Decision

In stark contrast to the disappointing report of the ten spies, were the reports of the two men of faith: Caleb and Joshua. The people listened to the report of the majority. It just seemed the natural and reasonable thing to do. The people gave no credibility or just did not want to consider what Caleb and Joshua had seen. So the majority ruled here; but the majority was wrong! I might interject this: the minority plus God always makes for what is right.

The question arises: To whom do you listen? Believers should listen to God and not to man. When someone questions what you are doing for the Lord, go to God and talk with Him about it. Now, I'm not saying that you should never consider the advice of another person; but what I am saying is, when the time comes for drawing a conclusion of the matter, having prayed about that matter, and having given God the time to lead you in the way you should go, act with confidence and in faith. **James 1:5 – 8**.

One more thing: Never have your mind made up before you pray to God about a matter; be sure that you have a clean and sensitive spirit about you. If you do this, God will always lead you in the right decision and in the right path to take. **Isaiah 30:21**: *"Your ears shall hear a word behind you, saying, 'This is the way, walk in it.' "* **NKJV**.

What is happening here?

The children of Israel definitely do not have a sensitive spirit about them, and <u>they have a conclusion already in mind</u>: Wrong decision. They have <u>refused to go and possess the Promised Land</u>: Wrong decision. They have <u>rebelled against the leadership of God's chosen men</u> - Moses, Aaron, Caleb and Joshua: Wrong decision. They are actively engaged in the process of <u>making plans to return to Egypt</u>: Wrong decision. They definitely have a bent to making wrong decisions! *"Let us choose a leader and go back to Egypt."* **Verse 4 ESV**.

The children took the wrong choice to begin with, and they then made an additional wrong choice by disobeying God's warning again. They were embarrassed more than sorry for their sins. They were sorry that their sin was discovered and had been openly made known.   They did not want to suffer from the consequence of their wrong decisions. **Verses 39 – 45**.

What is the result of all these sins of rebellion?   God expresses His disgust with them; His longsuffering has now come to an end. *"The Lord is longsuffering and abundant in mercy, forgiving iniquity and transgression; but He by no means clears the guilty, visiting the iniquity of the fathers on the children to the third and fourth generation."* **Verse 18 NKJV**.

God displays His disgust: *"How long shall I bear with <u>this evil congregation</u> who complain against Me? <u>I have heard the complaints which the children of Israel make against Me."</u>* **Verse 27 NKJV**. Their sin was not only against Moses and the faithful; their great sin was against God Himself.   God is longsuffering and not willing that any should perish, as we read in **2 Peter 3:9**, but His longsuffering is not eternal. It has a limit, and the children of Israel have crossed that line. We call such actions <u>"trespasses,"</u> in that these actions have crossed the line. We call such actions <u>"sins"</u> or missing the mark of the glory of God.

In **Verse 29** God uses strong words in making their fate known: *". . . As I live, says the Lord, just as you have spoken in My hearing, so I will do to you: The carcasses of you who have complained against Me shall fall in this wilderness, all of you who were numbered, according to your entire number, from twenty years old and above."* **NKJV**.

All those that were 20 years old and older will die in the wilderness. The number of years that they would spend wandering and dying in the wilderness was one year for every day that they spied out the land. The expedition team spent 40 days surveying the land; therefore, they would wander 40 years. **Verse 34:** *"According to the number of days in which you spied out the land, forty days, for each day you shall bear your guilt one year, namely forty years, and you shall know my rejection."* **NKJV**.

Notice the original excuse the children of Israel used for their rebellion in **Verses 2 & 3**: *"And all the children of Israel complained against Moses and Aaron, and the whole congregation said to them, "if only we had died in the land of Egypt! Or if only we had died in this wilderness! Why has the Lord brought us to this land to **fall by the sword, that our wives and children should become victims? Would it not be better for us to return to Egypt?**"* The complainers were the victims of rebellion, and the children would be the victors of obedience. *"But your little ones, whom you said would be victims, I will bring in, (victors) and they shall know the land which you have despised."* **Verse 31 NKJV**.

It is worth noting that God had not mentioned Moses and Aaron as being among those who would enter the Promised Land. Why were their names not included here with the names of Caleb and Joshua? Though Moses and Aaron had not disqualified themselves yet, they would later. God already knew that they would sin soon and be forbidden to enter the Promised Land. If He included them here, it would seem as though God was later surprised by the actions of Moses and Aaron. God is all knowing.

These rebels would try to make things right, but in their attempt they would disobey God's word. It was too late. The rebels took up arms and attacked the Amalekites and the Canaanites; and their attempt was futile. *"Then the Amalekites and the Canaanites who dwelt in that mountain came down and attacked them, and drove them back as far as Hormah."* **Verse 45 NKJV**.

Chapter 15

Laws

God is to be worshipped with a pure and clean heart. That was not just true in the days of old; it remains true today. Things change, but God never changes. There is an old Gospel Song, written by <u>Red Foley</u> that states: *"Time has made a change in me."*

The children of Israel have sinned greatly, and God has sentenced them to death. One by one they would die the wilderness over a 40-year period. This death would be a slow one; and with the coming of each new, hot, and humid day, they would be reminded of their disobedience and rebellion. However, they would still fall to that besetting sin of complaining.

Those twenty years old and above would slowly die in the wilderness as a result of their sin; but God has not forgotten those who would be entering the land, and He gives to them His detailed requirements concerning the sacrifices that were to be made upon arrival.

The first fruits belong to the Lord. . . . *"<u>When you come into the land</u> you are to inhabit, which I am giving you, and <u>you offer to the Lord from the herd or from the flock a food offering or a burnt offering or a sacrifice, to fulfill a vow or as a freewill offering or at your appointed feasts</u>, to <u>make a pleasing aroma to the Lord</u>, . . . and when you eat of the bread of the land, you shall present a contribution to the Lord."* **Verses 2 – 3 & 19 ESV**.

God now gives to Moses His laws and the required sacrifices that are to be made for sins that were committed unintentionally, as well as presumptuous sins. Sometimes a person may sin against God unintentionally or unwittingly. We understand that; but what are presumptuous sins? The literal meaning of presumptuous sin is *"with a high hand,"* or perhaps I could say, intentional and premeditated sin committed with an aggressive attitude with fist raised before the Lord in defiance of His commands.

Presumptuous sins are sins that are knowingly committed; a person knows that a deed is sin, but he commits it anyway in direct defiance of God. It could be something that a person considers small, or it could be something understood to be grievous. All sins are grievous sins to the holy God.

God first deals with unintentional sins. *"But if you sin unintentionally, and do not observe all these commandments that the Lord has spoken to Moses, all that the Lord has commanded you by Moses, from the day that the Lord gave commandment, and onward throughout your generations, then if it was done unintentionally without the knowledge of the congregation, all the congregation shall offer one bull from the herd for a burnt offering, a pleasing aroma to the Lord, ..."* **Verses 22 – 24 ESV**.

God cannot allow any sin to go unpunished. There must be an atonement made for all sin. There is an expression that we use that can be compared to this sin: *"Ignorance of the law is no excuse."* Now if sinful man has such a requirement for crimes against the law, isn't it is obvious that a holy God would have an even greater requirement?

What is the remedy for unintentional sin? It is the same thing that is required for intentional sin. *"And according to the law almost all things are purified with blood, and without shedding of blood there is no remission."* **Hebrews 9:22 NKJV**.

The great news for believers is that the holy sacrifice of Jesus and the shedding of His precious blood takes away all sin, known and unknown. *"But if we are living in the light of God's presence, just as Christ is, then we have fellowship with each other, and the blood of Jesus, His Son, cleanses us from every sin."* **1 John 1:7 NLT**.

Presumptuous sin displays a despising of God's Word. **Verse 31**. The presumptuous sin here is the violation of the Sabbath. Look at this sin: the man was gathering sticks on the Sabbath. **Verse 32**. One might say, that seems to be such a trivial thing. But God is holy, His Word is holy, and He calls His Sabbath holy. God is not trivial; He is holy. Yes, the Sabbath was made for man and not God, but man must be obedient to God's demands. God demands that we keep the Sabbath holy.

Look at the punishment of this infraction: Death by stoning. **Verse 36**. It's not the deed here; it is the defiance of God by this man who presumptuously, knowingly, and aggressively disobeyed God. He did it openly, he did it defiantly, and he did it without fear or reverence for the word of God.

Should God overlook such an attitude? No, He should not! Many unbelievers show such defiance to God today, and it appears that their actions go unpunished. But they, as is the man here, have been "placed under guard." They have not gotten away with anything. They are awaiting the Great White Throne Judgment. **Revelation 20: 11 – 15**.

God is never mocked without the mocker being punished. However, God moves in His own timing. All people will answer for every thought and action against God at the Great White Throne Judgement. The punishment will be eternal and grievous.

There is an unusual command given by God here. That commandment concerns blue tassels on the corners of one's outer garment. **Verses 37 – 41**.

What is the significance of these blue tassels? It is to serve as a reminder to the children of Israel that they are to serve and obey all of God's commands.

Perhaps I might compare it to the old saying: *"Tie a string around your finger to remind you to do something."* When they saw the blue tassel, it would be a continual reminder.

It is good to be reminded, and it is better to be faithful in doing the thing for which you need to be reminded to do.

Chapter 16

More Rebellion

My first thought is: Will these people ever learn? No, they will not. Now we have 250 men, a small army, rising up against Moses and Aaron, who are led by the Levite priest Korah and his two buddies Dathan and his brother On. Now Korah was a Kohath priest who was responsible for the care of the furniture inside the Holy Place and the Holy of Holies. Apparently Korah felt he was special, and he had great influence over the two brothers Dathan and On.

Moses makes known what the actual reason for the rebellion of Korah and his buddies actually is in **Verses 9 – 11**: *"Does it seem a small thing to you that the <u>God of Israel has chosen you</u> from among all the people of Israel to be near Him as you serve in the Lord's Tabernacle and to stand before the people to minister to them? <u>He has given this special ministry to you and your fellow Levites,</u> <u>but now you are demanding the priesthood as well!</u> The one you are really revolting against is the Lord! <u>And who is Aaron that you are complaining about him?</u>"* **NLT**.

Korah, Dathan, and On rebel against Moses and Aaron's leadership. They have committed trespasses against God, or they have "stepped over the line" against God's will.

So, Korah, Dathan, On and their fellow anarchists want more esteem, or to be seen as equal to <u>Moses as leader</u> and <u>Aaron as the High Priest</u>; or to state it more correctly, given more glory. The sin was <u>pride</u>, and pride goes just before destruction, and the pride is fanned with <u>a haughty spirit</u>, Solomon writes. **Proverbs 16:18**. I like how Eugene Peterson phrases the attitude of Korah: *"Getting on his high horse."* **Verse 2, The Message**. I could say that they viewed themselves as legends in their own eyes. The Apostle Paul warns the believer in **Romans 12:3:** *"For I say, through the grace given to me, to everyone who is among you, not to think of himself more highly that he ought to think, but to think soberly, as God has dealt to each one a measure of faith."* **NKJV**.

This threesome also had great influence over many others; and they apparently had been complaining about Moses and Aaron behind their back with about 250 fellow grumblers of the people.

Now it is important to take note that Korah and his fellow protesters were already serving in the Tabernacle, therefore, they were among those who were above 20 years old whom God had just condemned to die in the wilderness; and they would be among the first to die because of disobedience and rebellion. Remember that a Levite had to be <u>at least 25 years of age</u> before he could begin his training as a priest, and not until he was 30 could he begin his ministry, **Numbers 8:23 – 26**.

What was the result of this uprising? Korah continued to complain and fan dissention among the people all the way to the time of God pouring out His wrath, **Verse 19**. As the protesters stood at the door of the Tabernacle with censers in hands, with their wives and their children at their side, a huge sinkhole opened up with fire belching from it and swallowed and consumed Korah, Dathan, On, their families, and the 250 fellow complainers with fire, **Verses 31 – 35**.

The son of Aaron was commanded by God to retrieve the bronze censers from the fiery pit; and to hammer them into a sheet of bronze to be a cover for the Bronze Altar of Burnt Offering. **Verses 37 - 40**.

The truth that is contained in these verses is that every servant of God must be careful not to see what others are doing for the Lord as better than his own calling; each servant of God must concentrate upon the special ministry that God has called him to do. God only called you to your ministry, and He had no other person in mind for your ministry.

Did you know that God does not make duplicates or clones? When He makes anything, it is a special masterpiece and it is like no other; it is one of a kind.

So when God calls you to a ministry, He calls a special person, to a special place, to do a special thing. Don't look at others; look at what God has given you to do, where you are, and use the tools that He has provided for you to use.

Give it all that you have, and you will be happy in life, you will have a special purpose in life, and you will be a special blessing in the lives of others.

Now, one would think that God had made His point clear to the people, but that was not the case. On the very next day after God judges Korah and his followers, "all the people" of the congregation complain that Moses and Aaron have unjustly killed Korah and the 250 priests. **Verse 41**. But this was not the doing of Moses and Aaron; it was the judgment of God by the hand of God.

This continual revolting greatly angered God, and though Moses and Aaron try to make atonement for the people, it is too late for the wrath of God had already begun. **Verse 46**.

Still, the commitment of Aaron is seen as he stands with the incense of atonement between the people and God's plague. God honors the commitment of Aaron and Moses and stops the plague. But 14,700 people have already died from the plague.

God honors the commitment of His servants. Always be faithful to intercede for others. God will honor your faithfulness.

Chapter 17

Aaron's Rod

God judges leaders with a greater punishment than the normal believer; God expects more from those to whom He has given more. **Luke 12:48**. With greater responsibility comes greater expectations. God is about to do a great miracle here with the staff of Aaron, and He will have the miracle staff of Aaron placed into the Ark of the Covenant as a memorial to the people.

Why is God doing this miracle? It is because the leadership of Moses and Aaron has been questioned over and over again. Therefore, God now makes an undeniable confirmation of just who He has called to be His high priest.

In this chapter we have the budding of Aaron's staff, or rod. A staff and rod had great significance. The staff was carved from a hardwood tree, and the owner of the staff had carried it throughout his life. The staff represents the owner. It was not a green piece of wood, but aged, hard, weathered, dried, and void of the ability to produce another tree.

The walking staff was an undeniable possession of a person; this is seen when the staff of Judah was taken by Tamar as proof of an agreement. **Genesis 38:18**. A staff was used not only as a walking support, but as a weapon for protection, and as is seen here, as a priestly and royal symbol of authority.

God asks for the staff of each of the twelve tribal leaders to be inscribed with the name of the owner, brought to Moses, and then Moses was to place all twelve staffs upon the floor of the Tabernacle of Meeting, where they would be kept overnight.

The proof of divine chosen leadership would be the staff that has blossomed on the next day. **Verse 5**. On the next day Moses entered the Tabernacle and retrieved the budding rod of Aaron. But it not only had leaves and flowers blooming from it, but it also had mature almonds that were ready to eat upon the staff. **Verse 8**: *"On the next day Moses went into the tent of the testimony, and behold, <u>the staff of Aaron for the house of Levi had sprouted and put forth buds and produced blossoms, and it bore ripe almonds</u>."* **ESV.**

Why did God have Moses take the staff or rod of Aaron back into the Tabernacle and place it inside the Ark of the Covenant for safe keeping? It was because the grumbling people would continue to grumble and question the leadership of God's chosen man and God Himself.

The well-known evangelist Billy Graham made this observation: *"Grumbling and gratitude are, for the child of God, in conflict. Be grateful and you won't grumble. Grumble and you won't be grateful."* **Billy Graham**

The besetting sin of the children of Israel is the same as believers of today. They are eager to be engaged in grumbling, and resistant to acknowledging and being thankful for God's blessing. They are void of gratitude.

When people think of you, I hope that they think of a thankful, happy, gracious, loving, caring, and obedient person. If that is true, then you have been a budding memorial of the goodness and grace of God to others. As the budding staff of Aaron was kept as a memorial to the people of God's leadership, may your life be such a budding reminder.

The encouraging Gospel song of Steve Green, "<u>Find us Faithful</u>," proclaims:

"We're pilgrims on the journey of the narrow road,

And those who've gone before us line the way.

Cheering on the faithful, encouraging the weary.

Their lives a stirring testament to God's sustaining grace.

Surrounded by so great a cloud of witnesses,

Let us run the race not only for the prize.

But as those who've gone before us,

Let us leave to those behind us,

The heritage of faithfulness,

passed on through godly lives.

O may all who come behind us find us faithful, ...

After all our hopes and dreams have come and gone,

And our children sift through all we've left behind.

May the clues that they discover,

and the memories they uncover,

Become the light that leads them,

to the road we each must find.

O may all who come behind us find us faithful,

May the fire of our devotion light their way.

May the footprints that we leave,

Lead them to believe,

And the lives we live inspire them to obey.

O may all who come behind us find us faithful.

Steve Green

Chapter 18

Priestly Duties

The priests bear the responsibility of the Sanctuary. What does that mean? It means that priests are responsible for keeping the Sanctuary holy and pure, because it represents God, and they represent God as well. There is a great responsibility that comes with representing God and in being His child.

Parents often challenge their children to, "Remember whose you are!" When people see children, they think about the parents. The honor of the parents is at stake with the actions of their children.

This is true with the children of Israel; when others see them, they think of God. The priests were responsible to bear any offense that might reflect impurity upon the place of worship.

God wants us to keep ourselves pure in life and to be pure in our worship of Him in His earthly sanctuary, or the church. Today, every believer is a *"royal priesthood"*: *"But you are a chosen generation, a royal priesthood, a holy nation, His own special people, that you may proclaim the praises of Him who called you out of darkness into His marvelous light, who once were not a people but are now the people of God, who had not obtained mercy but now have obtained mercy."* **1 Peter 2:9 & 10 NKJV**.

Peter goes on to write that as a royal priesthood, and travelers in life, believers are to behave honorably, in such a manner that our good and honorable works are clearly seen. Yes, believers are responsible for the honor of God. The Apostle Paul writes that the body of a believer is <u>the Temple of God</u>. **1 Corinthians 6:19 & 20**: *"Or do you not know that <u>your body is the temple of the Holy Spirit who is in you, whom you have from God, and you are not your own</u>? For you were bought at a price; therefore glorify God in your body and in your spirit, which are God's."* **NKJV**.

There is another point to be made here. Jesus is our High Priest and He has born the sins of the world; He is responsible for the atonement of the sins of the believer:

- **Hebrews 4:14 – 16**, *". . . For we do not have a High Priest who cannot sympathize with our weaknesses, but was in all points tempted as we are, yet without sin. . . ."*

- **Hebrews 8:1 – 6**, *". . . We have such a High Priest, who is seated at the right hand of the throne of the Majesty in heavens, a Minister of the sanctuary and of the true tabernacle which the Lord erected, and not man. . . ."* **NKJV**.

- **Hebrews 9:11 – 15**, *"But Christ came as High Priest of the good things to come, with the greater and more perfect tabernacle not made with hands, that is, not of this creation. . . . And for this reason He is the Mediator of the new covenant, by means of death, for the redemption of the transgression under the first covenant, that those who are called may receive the promise of the eternal inheritance."* **NKJV**

- **2 Corinthians 5:21**, *"For He made Him who knew no sin to be sin for us, that we might become the righteousness of God in Him."* **NKJV**.

We also read that God held Aaron personally responsible for the tithes of the people. **Verses 8 – 24**. <u>The people had a responsibility also, and that was for the support of the Priesthood</u>. The Levites were not given an inheritance of the Promised Land. They were charged with the spiritual welfare of the people and for the house of God.

The sacrifices that were offered fed the priests and their families. The tithes that were brought to the Tabernacle were to be used in securing any extra need that the priest might have.

- *"Every devoted thing in Israel shall be yours."* **Verse 14 NKJV**.

- *"Behold I have given the children of Levi all the tithes in Israel as an inheritance in return for the work which they perform, the work of the tabernacle of meeting."* **Verse 21 NKJV**.

The priests were not exempt from tithing. They were also commanded to give a tithe of the tithes that they received from the people to the Lord. **Verse 26**: *And the Lord spoke to Moses, saying, "Moreover, you shall speak and say to the Levites, 'When you take from the people of Israel the tithe that I have given you from them for your inheritance, <u>then you shall present a contribution from it to the Lord, a tithe of the tithe</u>."* **ESV**.

The priests truly were a royal priesthood, and to whom much is given, much is required. **Luke 12:48**: *". . . For everyone to whom much is given, from him much will be required; and to whom much has been committed, of him they will ask the more."* **NKJV**.

Child of God, be careful how you live. Take care of the things in which you have been given responsibility, and give your all to the Lord!

Jesus is our Supreme Example, and we are the visible example of a child of God to those around us. Make it your aim in life to be a faithful priest of God.

Chapter 19

Purification Laws

We have here recorded the significance of a perfect <u>red heifer</u> as the chosen sacrifice and whose ashes were to be sprinkled upon a person who has come into contact with a dead person or animal.

When Jesus was upon this earth, He touched the dead and give them new life. When a person asks forgiveness of his sin, the blood of Jesus then becomes the purification and atonement for that person, and the Father makes that believer a new creation and brings him into eternal life. Jesus is life; sin is death. Jesus is light and sin is darkness.

The two methods that were used in cleansing are:

1. Water

2. Waiting.

The sacrifice was to be perfect. The sacrifice was to be slaughtered *"outside the camp."* The blood of the red heifer was to be sprinkled at the entrance of the Tabernacle. The sacrifice was to be burned upon the Altar of Burnt Offering. Cedar, hyssop, and a scarlet thread are to be thrown into the fire as the red heifer is being burned. (That single scarlet thread, compared by some as the <u>*scarlet thread of redemption,*</u> can be traced all throughout scripture.) The ashes of the offering were to be mixed with water. This holy water mixture was to be kept in the Tabernacle to be used in sprinkling upon any person who might come into contact with any dead body.

The person who has been sprinkled with the holy water would not be considered clean until evening. **Verse 22**: *"Whatever the unclean person touches shall be unclean; and the person who touches it shall be unclean until evening."* **NKJV**.

There is some significance with this offering and the believer. Jesus is the only purification for sin. In **Acts 4:12**: *"Nor is there salvation in any other, for there is no other name under heaven given among men by which we must be saved."* **NKJV**.

Only one way, only one salvation, only one sacrifice; only one God.

Be a clean vessel for God; if you are, everyone who comes into contact with you will be influenced by the good hand of God.

One of my favorite worship songs is "One Pure and Holy Passion," written by Passion Music. Some of the lyrics are:

One Pure and Holy Passion

Give to me one pure and holy passion,

Give to me one magnificent obsession,

Give to me one glorious ambition for my life,

To know and follow hard after you.

To know and follow hard after you,

To go as Your disciple in the truth,

This world is empty, pale, and poor,

Compared to knowing you my Lord.

Lead me on and I will run and follow you.

Chapter 20

Striking the Rock

In this chapter Moses is writing about the third part of the wandering of the children of Israel in the wilderness. After the calling of Moses and his returning to Egypt to lead the children of Israel out of captivity, three important segments can be seen:

1. From the Red Sea to Sinai: **Exodus 13 – 19**

2. From Sinai to Kadesh: **Numbers 11 & 12**

3. From Kadesh to Moab: **Numbers 20:1 – 22:1**.

In this chapter we read of death, failure, disobedience, and misfortune: The sister of Moses, <u>Miriam, dies</u>; <u>Moses and Aaron disobey God</u>, and <u>Israel is not granted permission to travel the short route through Edom</u> on the way to possessing the Promised Land, and <u>Aaron dies</u>, who is the brother of Moses and the first High Priest of Israel.

They say bad news comes in three's; and we have not three but four very bad things. The truth is this: "Bad things happen to good people because we live in a bad world, controlled by Satan and his buddies. This world is not good; it is bad. People are not basically good; they are foundationally bad. People are born sinners and into a world of sin. *"For <u>all have sinned and fall short of the glory of God</u>,"* **Romans 3:23 NKJV**.

"Therefore, just as through one man sin entered the world, and death through sin, and thus <u>death spread to all men, because all sinned</u>." **Romans 5:12 NKJV**.

These two chapters (20 and 21) record what happened in the last year, or last two years of Israel's wanderings. Most likely this is the 40th year; and almost all of those whom God condemned to death in the wilderness have died; (**Numbers 14:26 – 38**: *"... The carcasses of you who have complained against Me shall fall in this wilderness, all of you who were numbered, according to your entire number, from twenty years old and above. Except for Caleb the son of Jephunneh and Joshua the son of Nun, you shall by no means enter the land which I swore I would make you dwell in. But your little ones, whom you said would be victims, I will bring in, and they shall know the land which you have despised...)* **NKJV**.

Moses is 119 years old at this time and in the last third of his amazing life. Stephen speaks of Moses in his message to the high priests which is recorded by Luke in **Acts 7:17 – 36**: *"... Now <u>when he was forty years old</u>, it came into his heart to visit his brethren, the children of Israel... Then, ... Moses fled and became a dweller in the land of Midian, where he had two sons.... <u>And when forty years had passed</u>, an Angel of the Lord appeared to him in a flame of fire in a bush, in the wilderness of Mount Sinai. ... He brought them out, after he had shown wonders and signs in the land of Egypt, and in the Red Sea, <u>and in the wilderness forty years</u>."* **NKJV**.

<u>Moses lived 120 years</u>, and then God ended his life on Mount Nebo. **Deuteronomy 34:5 – 7**: *"So Moses the servant of the Lord died there in the land of Moab, according to the word of the Lord. And He buried him in a valley in the land of Moab, opposite Beth Peor; but no one knows his grave to this day. Moses was one hundred and twenty years old when he died. His eyes were not dim nor his natural vigor diminished."* **NKJV**.

The life of Moses can be capsuled in three equal sections:

1. From birth to his exile in Median: <u>40 years</u>.

2. From his exile in Median to the crossing of the Red Sea: <u>40 years</u>.

3. From the crossing of the Red Sea to his death: <u>40 years</u>.

Having reached Kadesh, as we read in this chapter, Israel asks permission of passage through the land of the Edom (the descendants of Esau). However, Edom refused passage and stationed an army before Israel in resistance. Because of this refusal of passage, Moses turns the people around and travels about 100 miles back to Mount Hor. *"Then he said, 'You shall not pass through.' So Edom came out against them with many men and with a strong hand. <u>Thus Edom refused to give Israel passage through his territory; so Israel turned away from him.</u> Now the children of Israel, the whole congregation, journeyed from Kadesh and came to Mount Hor."* **Verses 20 – 22 NKJV**.

Having reached Mount Hor, which is at the border of the land of Edom, God ends the life of Aaron, the brother of Moses and Israel's first high priest. **Verses 23 – 29**.

God has already made it clear to everyone that Moses and Aaron would not be granted permission to enter the Promised Land because of his same sin of disobedience when Moses strikes the rock twice. Aaron was also guilty by having the same attitude as Moses and going along with him. **Verses 10 – 12**.

God declares openly to the children of Israel that the son of Aaron, <u>Eleazar, is to be the successor of Aaron as High Priest</u>. The high priestly clothing is then placed upon Eleazar before all the people. **Verses 28 & 29**.

Let's consider a few things relating to these events.

<u>Miriam dies of old age</u>. She was beloved but she had also been rebellious to her brother Moses and God. She felt that she and Aaron were equal to Moses in leadership. Their thoughts of the heart were brought to the forefront by their unacceptance of Moses' Ethiopian wife. **Numbers 12:1 & 2**.

All that is written of the death of Miriam is: *"... and <u>Miriam died there and was buried</u> there."* **Verse 1 NKJV**. That is significant but there is no reference to her of any position of leadership.   Don't look at the ministry of others, just concentrate upon the ministry that God has given you. Press toward the mark of the calling of God in your life. **Philippians 4:14**.

Moses and Aaron allow the continual complaining of the people to limit their ministry, **Verses 2 – 13**. Miriam has died and her death was painful to Moses and Aaron; and then the people begin to complain.

Now it is understandable that the people were thirsty. It was reasonable that they wanted God to give them water; He had done so at <u>Marah</u>, **Exodus 15:22 – 25**, and in the <u>Wilderness of Sin</u>, **17:1 – 7**. But here at <u>Meribah,</u> God's anger was not with the complaining of the people for water, it was with the disobedience of Moses and Aaron. Though they had seen the hand of God in the past, they neglected to revere the holy hand of God. When anything is added to holiness, it contaminates it.

Moses and Aaron have had all they can take and they want vengeance upon the people. *"So Moses and Aaron went from the presence of the assembly to the door of the tabernacle of meeting, and they fell on their faces. And the glory of the Lord appeared to them."* **Verse 6 NKJV**.

We do not see that God is angry with the people. He wants to give them the water that they need. **Verses 7 & 8**. Though the people were complaining, we see <u>Moses full of anger,</u> as well as Aaron. The words of Moses were not the words of the holy God; Moses says: *"Listen you bunch of rebels! He shouted. Must we bring you water from this rock?' Then Moses raised his hand and struck the rock twice with the staff, and water gushed out. So all the people and their livestock drank their fill."* **Verses 10 - 11 NLT.**

What was the sin here? Well, there were many. We see trespasses by Moses and Aaron, or crossing the line. Moses and Aaron were presumptuous of the voice of God, and they took liberties here. They went beyond what God had given them to do.

What did God ask of Moses and Aaron? God told Moses to take the rod (it could have been Moses' rod or it could have been Aaron's rod that was housed in the Tabernacle), and Moses was to speak to the rock.

The rod symbolized divine authority, and the voice of Moses was the divine instrument that God chose to be used. So, Moses obeyed God in two ways:

1. He called all the people together.

2. He took the rod.

However, Moses and Aaron had not put away bitterness. Moses spoke out of anger and acted in disobedience. Moses and Aaron desired wrath, and their added desire merely added to the clamor with a malicious temper.

What Moses and Aaron did not have was the kindness of God, the forgiving spirit of God, and they were void of the love of God. **Ephesians 4:25 – 32.** Moses failed the people; and he failed God by striking the rock not once, but twice, and struck it in anger.

The Apostle Paul writes in **1 Corinthians 10:4**: *"and all drank the same spiritual drink. For they drank of the spiritual*

Rock that followed them, and that Rock was Christ." **NKJV**. Yes, the Rock here in the wilderness that gushed forth refreshing and life preserving water for the people was Jesus.

Some important truths for leaders are:

- Do not allow the sins of others to pull you into some rash and presumptuous sin; do not rush to judgment.

- Never go beyond what God has given you to do.

- When asking God for wisdom and guidance, do not put in your "two cents worth."

Now, did Moses and Aaron believe God? Well, yes they did in most ways, but here God Himself says this of Moses and Aaron: *"Then the Lord spoke to Moses and Aaron, 'Because you did not believe Me, to hallow Me in the eyes of the children of Israel, therefore you shall not bring this assembly into the land to which I have given them.' "* **Verses 12 & 13 NKJV.**

Moses and Aaron tainted the holy name of God; and they acted in anger, wrath and vengeance rather than belief with the mercy of God, the grace of God, and the love of God.

The chapter is brought to a close with the mentioning that at the death of Aaron, the people mourned his death for thirty days.

Eleazar now takes the divine mantle of the high priesthood.

Chapter 21

The Bronze Serpent

Having been traveling through the wilderness for <u>forty years</u>, the presence of Israel is becoming well known to the people in Canaan and the Sinai peninsula; and the children of Israel would experience great resistance by the nations that lived there. The miracles that God had done for them were well known by all.

Remember, there are about two to three million Israelites marching through the wilderness. That is a significant number of people; and on top of that, Israel has a standing army of over six hundred thousand men ready to fight. One can easily see the fear that these nations must have had. But God is going to judge these nations, and these people, by Israel and out of His righteous judgment.

The Canaanite king Arad took up arms against Israel, and he and his army were slaughtered by Israel.

Notice that the Hebrew name that was given to the battle field was *"Hormah,"* which means *destruction* or *slaughter.* **Verse 3**, **NKJV**: *"And the Lord listened to the voice of Israel and delivered up the Canaanites, and <u>they utterly destroyed them and their cities</u>. So the name of that place was called Hormah."*

The destruction was not be by the might of Israel, but by the mighty and awesome hand of God. Israel has just prayed for God to deliver them, and if He would deliver them, they would *"utterly destroy"* the cities.

What does "utterly destroy" mean? It means that everything related with the city would be destroyed. The difficult thought here is that even *"the women and children were destroyed."*

Deuteronomy 2:34: *"We took all his cities at that time, and <u>we utterly destroyed the men, women, and little ones of every city; we left none remaining.</u>"* **NKJV**.

We find this *"utter destruction"* pronouncement by God many times as the children of Israel took possession of the Promised Land and at other times. King Saul was commanded by God to utterly destroy Agag, king of the Amalekites, in **1 Samuel 15:2 & 3**: *"Thus says the Lord of hosts: '<u>I will punish Amalek for what he did to Israel, how he ambushed him on the way when he came up from Egypt. Now go and attack Amalek, and utterly destroy all that they have, and do not spare them. But kill both man and woman, infant and nursing child, ox and sheep, camel and donkey.</u>' "* **NKJV**.

God is the righteous judge in all things. He judges all things with holy actions, and His judgments are just. **Psalm 119:75**: *"I know, O Lord, that Your judgments are right, and that in faithfulness You have afflicted me."* **NKJV**; **Revelation 19:2**: *"For true and righteous are His judgments. . . "* **NKJV**.

King Saul did not completely obey God and spared Agag and the best of the land. King Saul was punished by God for his disobedience. Remember, <u>partial obedience, is complete disobedience</u>. You cannot "almost obey God." God demands "complete obedience." It is not ours to question the demands of God. *"What shall we say then? <u>Is there unrighteousness with God? Certainly not! For He says to Moses, 'I will have mercy on whomever I will have mercy, and I will have compassion on whomever I will have compassion.</u>"* **Romans 9:14 & 15 NKJV**.

How are we to understand this *"utter destruction"*? First of all, we must trust the goodness of God. Now that statement seems out of place. However, with God there is no shadow of turning from unrighteousness with the good hand of God; and in judgment God shows no favoritism in His judgment or gifts, not even a shadow of turning; **James 1:17**. God is completely good, thoroughly loving, and faithfully just. One can be certain that God is always faithful to His word; **Isaiah 55:11**.

Standing in stark contrast to God, mankind is not basically good, he is fundamentally bad, evil, and sinful. Mankind needs redemption from his bad, evil, and sinful ways. God the Father sent His Only Begotten Son Jesus Christ to pay the demanded penalty for sin; and the penalty is death.

Now, the people here who were sentenced to *"total destruction"* were sentenced by God for their unacceptable and detestable sins. Israel was the sanctioned executioner of God's just judgment. **Romans 13:1 – 7**: *"Let <u>every soul be subject to the governing authorities. For there is no authority except from God, and the authorities that exist are appointed by God</u>. . . . For he is God's minister to you for good. But if you do evil, be afraid; for he does not bear the sword in vain; <u>for he is God's minister, an avenger to execute wrath on him who practices evil</u>. . . ."* **NKJV**.

This divine judgment and godly wrath cannot be clearly understood, but the decision to judge in wrath must be trusted to God alone.

Believers are not God's messengers of judgment; believers are God's messengers of Good News. Believers are not to be known for justice; they must be known for their Godly love, mercy, and grace. **John 3:16 – 18; 2 Peter 3:9**.

I find this passage difficult to get a solid understanding; so I put my trust in the Solid Rock of Jesus in whom I do have a solid understanding.

If there is anything good in this exercising of *"utter destruction"* that God demanded of Israel, it would be this:

Those children and babies that were destroyed had not reached the age of accountability and, therefore, they would be granted eternal life to live with God in His heaven. Their parents were pagans who did not trust God, and they would have raised their children to be pagans, not knowing God. Beyond that, I must trust the judgments of God.

Now, God's righteous judgments were sanctioned to be carried out by His chosen authorities. There are authorities and there are false authorities. Who are the false authorities? These authorities are the principalities, powers, and workers of iniquity at work against us in heavenly places. The Apostle Paul write of these in **Ephesians 6:12**. This group of workers gets their authority from Satan; they move under the power of Satan. These powerful forces use flesh and blood creations. They give them power to attack the workers of righteousness, the believers in Christ Jesus. The defense of the righteous comes from the power of The Holy Spirit.

To battle these forces of Satan, believers must take up the armament that God has provided for them. The battle belongs to God, and the defense belongs to the believer to stand, having on the armor of God, and to stand faithfully in the heat of battle. God is our strength: **Psalm 7:1 & Psalm 3:3**. Though many rise up against us, God is for us.

After this great conquest by the children of Israel at Mount Hor, where Aaron died, they continue their travels *"by the Way of the Red Sea."* This is the road that leads to the Red Sea and the reason that they were on that road was to go around the land of Edom, which they were not given permission to travel through. Perhaps many of the people thought that it would be good to return to Egypt. They had heard their parents speak of it as they were growing up, and all they really knew about life was this seemingly endless trek of wandering.

However, this wandering wasn't endless or hopeless wandering. It was judgmental wandering because of unbelief.

Those who were alive had a great hope and promise from God. They were the ones that have been chosen to enter the Promised Land, and they would possess it.

The children of Israel would suffer a great punishment for a threefold sin. We read in **Verse 5**: *"And the people <u>spoke against God</u>, and <u>against Moses</u>: "Why have you brought us up out of Egypt to die in the wilderness? <u>For there is no food and no water, and our soul loathes this worthless bread.</u>"* **NKJV**.

The children of Israel had sinned against God, they sinned against Moses, and they sinned against the provisions of God that came from His good hand.

They had not died in the wilderness, but many were about to die. There was both food and water, but they did not like the bread that God provided, and they were unthankful for the water that quenched their thirst that God had provided. These people were totally unthankful and resented God and His chosen leader Moses.

For this threefold sin, God sent a plague of "fiery serpents" into the camp that entered every tent with the hot bite of death; and a huge number within the camp had died, and many were about to die. **Verse 6**.

The people quickly come to their senses and confess their threefold sin: *"... 'We have sinned, for <u>we have spoken against the Lord and against you</u>; pray to the Lord that He take away the serpents from us.' So Moses prayed for the people."* **Verse 7**.

The remedy that God gave for the snake bite was an unusual one, and it would require an act of faith. God told Moses to cast a bronze serpent and put it on a pole. The promise of God was that anyone who would look at the serpent on the pole, they would live. **Verses 8 & 9**.

Jesus referred to this very instance when Nicodemus came to Him at night asking for understanding of the purpose of

Jesus coming to save one of eternal death. *"And as Moses lifted up the serpent in the wilderness, even so must the Son of Man be lifted up, that whoever believes in Him should not perish but have eternal life. For God so loved the world that He gave His only begotten Son, that whoever believes in Him should not perish but have everlasting life."* **John 3:14 – 16 NKJV**.

It wasn't the bronze snake that gave life. It had no power at all; it was God who healed them and gave them life and a future. The medical field has selected as its symbol, or icon, a serpent on a pole. The symbol is often called *"The Rod of Asclepius"* and *"Caduceus,"* the traditional symbol of Hermes. But the *"Bronze Serpent on a pole"* predates them all.

After this the children of Israel return in their trek to the Promised Land. They move to and camped at Oboth, Ije Abarim in Moab, in the valley of Zered, Arnon, Beer, (where Moses gave them water), Mattanah, Nahaliel, Bamoth, and Pisgah.

In their travel to the Promised Land, the children of Israel would have many battles: Among them were in <u>Moab</u>, king Sihon of the <u>Amorites</u>; and king Og of <u>Bashan</u>; Moses states that these wars were written in *"The Book of The Wars of The Lord."* This book is thought to be a collection of poems and writings about various battles and conquests as they moved to possessing the Promised Land. Some of these poems are written here in **Verses 14 – 30**.

The next tragic event is what the children of Israel would encounter with the king **Balak**, son of Zippor and king of the Midianite city of Bashan, and the Moabites their allied people.

I might remind you that Moses went to Midian as he escaped Egypt. His father-in-law Jethro, the father of Zipporah, was a Midian priest. **Exodus 2:15 – 25 & Exodus 18**.

Chapter 22

Balak and Balaam

The children of Israel have reached Moab and are at the banks of the Jordan River, just opposite Jericho. Their arrival has caused great fear among the residents of the area.

The situation here is that the Moabite king Balak, the son of Zippor, was frightened by the children of Israel. There are around three million of them, and he and the kings of the area saw them as a threat. **Verse 3:** *"And Moab was exceedingly afraid of the people because they were many, and Moab was sick with dread because of the children of Israel."* **NKJV**.

They have heard the accounts of how God was with them, sustained them, provided for them, and defended them. The answer to their fears seemed to be a divine curse of God upon the children of Israel; and so they called the local, well-known mystic, diviner, soothsayer, and sorcerer Balaam. The Moabites, Canaanites, and Midianites were idol worshippers.

Balaam was a well-known diviner and soothsayer who loved money and ministered for personal gain. Balaam lived near the Euphrates River in the town of Pethor. **Verses 5 & 6**: *"Then he sent messengers to Balaam the son of Beor <u>at Pethor, which is near the River in the land of the sons of his people</u>, to call him, saying: 'Look, a people has come from Egypt. See, they cover the face of the earth, and are settling next to me! Therefore <u>please come at once, curse this people for me</u>, for they are too mighty for me. <u>Perhaps I shall be able to defeat them and drive them out of the land, for I know that he whom you</u>*

<u>bless is blessed, and he whom you curse is cursed.</u>" **NKJV**. Balaam is being perceived by the Moabites and Midianites as a true prophet, but he is not.

Balaam is referred to several times in Scripture as being a preacher of false doctrine and greed and as being a stumbling block for those who desire to serve God honorably. He was an opportunist:

Jude 11: *"Like Balaam, they will do anything for money."* **NLT**;

Joshua 13:22: *"The children of Israel also killed with the sword Balaam the son of Beor, the soothsayer, among those who were killed by them."* **NKJV**;

2 Peter 2:15: *"They have forsaken the right way and gone astray, following the way of Balaam the son of Beor, who loved the wages of unrighteousness;"* **NKJV**;

Revelation 2:14: *"But I have a few things against you, because you have there those who hold the doctrine of Balaam, who taught Balak to put <u>a stumbling block before the children of Israel, to eat things sacrificed to idols, and to commit sexual immorality.</u>"* **NKJV**.

Balaam's God was profit; he worshipped money and pleasure. He had little or no conviction, and he straddled the fence on issues. He was lukewarm, and did not know God Almighty.

There are many so-called preachers today whose ministry is for themselves, just like Balaam. They preach a health, wealth, prosperity, and pleasure message, which was the same as Balaam. Beware of them, and flee from them.

We see that Balaam's donkey was more perceptive of the Lord God and His presence than Balaam was.

The kings seek out and hire Balaam to curse the children of Israel, **Verse 6**. This was not going to happen, although

Balaam wanted to do so but God prevented him. He asked the kings to wait until he consulted God about the matter. **Verse 8**.

As Balaam goes through his searching for answers, and we see here that God speaks to him in much the same way as He did with King Abimelech in **Genesis 20:3**. Here God asks Balaam: *"Who are these men with you?"* **Verse 9**. God then tells Balaam in no uncertain terms: *"You shall not go with them; you shall not curse the people, for they are blessed."* **Verse 12 NKJV**.

When God blesses a people, that blessing cannot be revoked, **Isaiah 55:11**.

When Balaam returns to Balak, he has bad news for him. In effect, he says to Balak and the other kings: "Go home! I cannot go with you! And God will not let me curse the children of Israel. Just deal with it the best you can." **Verse 14**.

Under pressure of the kings, Balaam agrees to give one more night to see if God would change His mind. But God does not change His mind about the cursing, however he does give Balaam permission to travel back with the kings. **Verse 20**

As Balaam travels to Moab, God sent an Angel to stand in the way; but only Balaam's donkey sees the Angel. Balaam beats the donkey three times for resisting him, but Balaam was resisting God, **Verses 22 – 30**.

The unbelievable happens here. God gives the donkey the ability to speak Balaam's native language; and the surprising thing to me is that when the donkey speaks, Balaam answers the donkey as though he has heard donkeys talk before. The donkey is speaking because God is angry with Balaam.

Why was God angry with Balaam here? It was because he was in the process of resisting God and disobeying God. **Verse**

32. We witness Balaam giving a deception to the kings, that God would change His mind and allow Balaam to curse Israel.

Finally God opens the eyes of Balaam and he sees the Angel of the Lord standing in the road blocking the way, **Verses 31 – 36**.

Never be a deceiver; always be a proclaimer of the Good News of God without apology. Never give up! Never give in! Never turn away from the leadership of God!

Chapter 23

Balaam's Prophecy

Four times Balaam will offer sacrifices to see if God would change His mind; and each time God refuses to allow Balaam to curse the children of Israel. The first two oracles of Balaam are here in <u>Chapter 23</u> and the remaining two oracles are in <u>Chapter 24</u>.

Two times Balaam asks Balak to build seven altars with seven bulls and seven rams to be sacrificed upon them. **Verses 1**, & **29**.

What are the major truths that are pointed out here, even by a greedy prophet?

- I will not curse what God has not cursed. **Verse 8**

- I will not denounce what God has not denounced. **Verse 8**

- <u>I must take heed to speak what the Lord has put in my mouth</u>. **Verse 12**

- "<u>God is not a man, that He should lie</u>, nor a son of man, that He should repent." **Verse 19**

- <u>God is faithful to His word</u>; what He says, He will do. **Verse 19**

- <u>God blesses and His blessing cannot be reversed</u>. **Verse 20**

What do we know about God?

<u>We know that God is Omnipotent</u>. He has complete power and that power is supreme power. There is no power that can come against Him.

<u>We know that God is Omnipresent</u>. He has the ability to be everywhere at the same time. There is no place where God is not; there is no time in which God has not been there; and there is no person to which God has not spoken. Often we speak of God being in *"The eternal now."* **Psalm 139**.

<u>We know that God is Omniscient,</u> or He knows all things and there is nothing that God does not know, and there was never a time in which He did not know it all.

<u>We know that God is immutable,</u> or He does not change. He does not change because He is supreme: knowing all things, having all things, and able to do all things. There is nothing left for change. "Jesus Christ is <u>the same</u> yesterday, today, and forever." **Hebrews 13:8 NKJV**.

<u>We know that God is Sovereign</u> in all things.

<u>We know that God will judge</u> the earth, the angels, and all creation in the end.

<u>We know that Jesus is the pure and final sacrifice for sin</u>.

Be sure to have a clear understanding of God; and with a clear understanding of God, live a clear, godly life before all people. Don't be a fence straddler, and be certain to have godly desires, godly works, and be a godly example before others. Never be a stumbling block.

Chapter 24

Balaam's Prophecy Continued

The final two oracles of Balaam are listed here in **Chapter 24**. Here the blessing of Israel is confirmed much to the displeasure of King Balak of Moab and the Amalekites.

In **Verse 2** we see the reason behind the blessing given by Balaam: *". . . and the Spirit of God came upon him."* **NKJV**. Did you know that God <u>can use</u> evil people, if He desires to do so, in bringing about His will? God uses kings and nations; He gives to them authority to <u>carry out the bad news of judgment</u> upon those who deserve it. God chose the believers to carry His Good News of forgiveness, grace, mercy, love, and redemption to those in need of it.

Here Balaam blesses Israel even more:

- He pronounces God's blessing upon Israel's homes; **Verse 5**; their fields, **Verse 6**; and He makes known God's blessing of divine power over nations and people, **Verses 7 – 9**.

- Predicts the coming of the Messiah, *"The Star"* out of *Jacob*, **Verse 17**.

- He speaks of the judgment upon Moab, Edom, Kenites, Asshur and Eger. **Verse 17 - 24**.

Notice in **Verse 7** *". . . .His king shall be higher than Agag, and his kingdom shall be exalted."* **NKJV**. We read of disobedient king Saul and God's judgment of death of the Amalekite king Agag documented in **1 Samuel 15:32 & 33**. Now, Agag is not necessarily a specific person. Agag is a title that Amalekite kings were called, such as Pharaoh in Egypt, Abimelech in Philistia, and Caesar in Rome.

The significance of Agag is the judgment of God upon the Moabites: *"Thus says the Lord of hosts: 'I will punish what Amalek did to Israel, how he ambushed him on the way when he came up from Egypt. Now go and attack Amalek, and utterly destroy all that they have, and do not spare them. But kill both man and woman, infant and nursing child, ox and sheep, camel and donkey.' "* **1 Samuel 15:3 & 4 NKJV**. There Samuel questioned the disobedience of king Saul: *"Now the Lord set you on a mission, and said, 'Go, and utterly destroy the sinners, the Amalekites, and fight against them until they are consumed.' Why then did you not obey the voice of the Lord? Why did you swoop down on the spoil, and do evil in the sight of the Lord?"* **Verses 18 - 19 NKJV**.

Be faithful in doing what God has called you to do, and don't focus on what you cannot do; focus on what God can do through you, His servant. Never fear anything or anyone that might come against you; focus on God who is for you.

Balaam had to do what God desired for him to do; and there was nothing that Balak could do to stop the plan of God.

Be confident of this truth: What God says, He will do. Isaiah writes of God: *"So shall My word be that goes forth from My mouth; It shall not return to Me void, but it shall accomplish what I please, and it shall prosper in the thing for which I sent it."* **Isaiah 55:11 NKJV**. The Apostle Paul writes: *". . . If God is for us, who can be against us?"* **Romans 8:31 NKJV**.

Chapter 25

Israel and Moab

Brazen sin, presumptuous and premeditated sin that is committed in rebellion and with total disrespect of God, is what has happened here. Now remember, Israel is camped at Acacia (meaning wood), also called Shittim, which was just the other side of the Jordan River, and they were ready to march upon and take possession of the Promised Land.

The sin is harlotry, idolatry, and idol worship. The root cause of the sin was their being around bad people. Israel is associating with and finding themselves greatly influenced by the idolatrous Moabites and Amalekites here.

These people have rejected God. King Balak tried to have God's people cursed, but that failed. What did not fail was "The enemy among us." Be certain of this: Bad company spoils good morals. The Apostle Paul writes, *"Do not be deceived: 'Evil company corrupts good habits.' "* **1 Corinthians 15:33 NKJV**.

Bad company is deceptive. They may be likable and seek to be around you, but they have evil desires and they desire to corrupt you. Bad company is controlled by principalities and powers and workers of iniquity in high places. **Ephesians 6:12**.

All throughout the 40 years of wandering through the wilderness, one thing that reigned supreme was the children of Israel's desire for the pagan Egypt and how they loved

Egypt's pagan worship. But God was about to complete His judgment upon the children of Israel who were condemned to die in the wilderness: those who were 20 years old and above at the time that Israel refused to possess the land at Paran. **Numbers 14:29 & 30**: *"The carcasses of you who have complained against me shall fall in this wilderness, all of you who were numbered, according to your entire number, from twenty years old and above. Except for Caleb the son of Jephunneh and Joshua the son of Nun, you shall by no means enter the land which I swore I would make you dwell in."* **NKJV**.

The sin of harlotry that was running through the camp, was associated with Baal worship. **Verse 3**. Baal was the Canaanite's fertility god or idol. Israel would continue to fall to the idol worship of Baal throughout all Old Testament history. Idol worship was Israel's besetting sin.

For this sin of harlotry and idol worship, God tells Moses to hang all the ringleaders in the sight of the people. **Verses 4 & 5**. With this hanging comes the wrath of God, which is evidenced by a plague that kills 24,000 Israelites on that very day. **Verse 9**.

What brought this sin to a head was when a Midianite woman, whose name was Cozbi the daughter of Zur, was brought into the sacred court of the Tabernacle by Zimri the son of Salu, one of the leaders of the tribe of Simeon. **Verses 14 & 15**.

In **Verse 6** the situation is established: *And behold, one of the people of Israel came and brought a Midianite woman to his family, in the sight of Moses and in the sight of the whole congregation of the people of Israel, while they were weeping in the entrance of the tent of meeting."* **ESV** and **Verses 14 & 15**.

The sin of these two was blatant, and it infuriated Phinehas, Aaron's grandson, the son of Eleazar the high priest. Phinehas was a priest, and in great wrath with overcoming zeal, he took a javelin and thrust it through both the Midianite woman and the Israelite, apparently in the very act of having sexual relations. **Verses 7 & 8**.

This quick act of judgment by Phinehas stopped the plague, but not before 24,000 people had died from the plague. This final plague finished off the last of those who had been condemned to die of the older generation, **Verse 9**.

I often wonder how a people who have been so blessed by God can so quickly turn away from God. This puzzles the mind, but it displays the danger of excessive association with of workers of darkness.

Don't listen to bad news more than you listen to God's Good News. Be involved in spreading the Good News and you will not have time for bad news.

James confirms this in **James 4:7 – 10**: *"Therefore submit to God. Resist the devil and he will flee from you. Draw near to God and He will draw near to you. Cleanse your hands, you sinners; and purify your hearts, you doubleminded. Lament and mourn and weep! Let your laughter be turned to mourning and your joy to gloom. Humble yourselves in the sight of the Lord, and He will lift you up."* **NKJV**.

Chapter 26

The Second Census

Now God has Moses to take a second census of the people, and they prepare for battle as they begin preparation for the possessing of the Promised Land.

The first census was taken on the first day of the second month, in the second year after the children of Israel had come out of the land of Egypt. This second census was taken in Moab at the Jordan River, just opposite Jericho. **Verse 4:** *"Take a census of the people, from twenty years old and upward, . . ."* **ESV**.

Let us take a look at the two censuses that were taken:

<table>
<tr><td><u>At Sinai</u></td><td><u>At Moab</u></td></tr>
<tr><td>Reuben: 46,500 men above 20</td><td>43,730 men above 20</td></tr>
<tr><td>Simeon: 59,300 men above 20</td><td>22,200 men above 20</td></tr>
<tr><td>Gad: 45,650 men above 20</td><td>40,500 men above 20</td></tr>
<tr><td>Judah: 74,600 men above 20</td><td>76,500 men above 20</td></tr>
<tr><td>Issachar: 54,400 men above 20</td><td>64,300 men above 20</td></tr>
<tr><td>Zebulun: 57,400 men above 20</td><td>60,500 men above 20</td></tr>
<tr><td>Manasseh: 32,200 men above 20</td><td>52,700 men above 20</td></tr>
<tr><td>Ephraim: 40,500 men above 20</td><td>32,500 men above 20</td></tr>
<tr><td>Benjamin: 35,400 men above 20</td><td>45,600 men above 20</td></tr>
</table>

Dan: 62,700 men above 20   64,400 men above 20

Asher: 41,500 men above 20   53,400 men above 20

Naphtali: 53,400 men above 20   45,400 men above 20

Total: 603,550 men above 20   601,730 men above 20

The **Levites a month old and older**:

22,000 males   23,000 males

What we see here is that over the 40 years of wandering in the wilderness there was a <u>decrease</u> of men above 20 years of age and able to fight; <u>a decrease of 1,820 men above 20</u>; and an <u>increase</u> in the number of Levites of 1,000 males who were over a month old. This census makes known the number of the army and the priests that would enter the Promised Land.

Everyone that was 20 years old and above at the taking of the first census had now died, with the exception of Caleb and Joshua. Moses would soon die.

It is important how one chooses to live his life. It is important whom one chooses as a companion. It is important whom one selects as a mentor; and it is important what one chooses for pleasure.

We only have one chance in life; therefore, make sure to choose to do the right thing. It is always right to make right decisions, regardless the repercussions. It is always wrong to make wrong decisions in fear of the repercussions that a right decision might create. Jesus is our example. He came to do the will of His Father, knowing in advance the repercussions.

The missionary Jim Elliot is famous for saying: *"He is no fool who gives what he cannot keep to gain what he cannot lose."* Remember that!

The Gospel song writer Lanny Wolfe wrote the song "ONLY ONE LIFE." The lyrics are:

"It matters so little how much you may own,

The places you've been or the people you've known.

For it all comes to nothing when placed at His feet;

It's nothing to Jesus, just memories to keep.

Only one life so soon it will pass,

Only what's done for Christ will last.

Only one chance to do His will,

So give to Jesus all your days,

It's the only life that pays,

When you recall you have but one life."

Lanny Wolfe

Chapter 27

Inheritance Laws

In this chapter we will see the loving heart of God and the appointment of Joshua as the successor of Moses, but first we see a problem that has presented itself. The problem was made known to Moses by the five daughters of Zelophehad.

As the children of Israel are at the brink of entering the Promised Land, great excitement is flowing through the camp; but there were some that had great concerns with regard to their future. One of those overlooked concerns is expressed by the daughters of Zelophehad.

Zelophehad is the great, great, great, great grandson of Joseph; and he was among those who had died in the wilderness because of the sin of disobedience, but not because of rebellion. Zelophehad had five daughters: Mahlah, Noah, Hoglah, Milcah, and Tirzah, but he had no sons. **Verse 1:** *"Then drew near the daughters of Zelophehad the son of Hepher, son of Gilead, son of Machir, son of Manasseh, from the clans of Manasseh the son of Joseph. The names of his daughters were: Mahlah, Noah, Hoglah, Milcah, and Tirzah."* **ESV**.

The problem here is inheritance and the secure future of not only these five women, but of all those women among the people who would be unable to receive an inheritance. They are unable to receive an inheritance merely because they are female and not male. The five daughters make their plea before Moses, and Moses asks God for direction in the matter. **Verse 2.**

"Why should the name of our father be removed from among his family because he had no son? Give us a possession among our father's brothers." **Verse 4 NKJV**.

These ladies have a valid point! This seems so wrong! And you know what? God said that it was wrong; this was not the desire of God. God will provide for these women and all other women who may have a similar situation. Remember this at all times: God does all things well! *"And they were astonished beyond measure, saying, 'He has done all things well. He makes both the deaf to hear and the mute to speak.'"* **Mark 7:37 NKJV**.

In **Verse 7** God says to Moses: *"The daughters of Zelophehad speak what is right; you shall surely give them a possession of inheritance among their father's brothers, and cause the inheritance of their father to pass to them."* **NKJV**.

The command of God was how the succession of heritage is to be carried out: to the son of the Father, the son of the father's brothers, and then to the son of the closest relative. **Verses 8 – 11**. We see an example of this through the kinsman redeemer, Boaz, in redeeming Naomi and Ruth in **Ruth 4:1 – 12**.

God leaves no one out. He provides for all His children. It is God's desire to bless all people and that all people would have equal opportunity of choosing their eternal future. In Chapter 36 the land inheritance is confirmed for them.

Jesus told His disciples just before He was to be crucified that He was going to prepare a place of inheritance for all of them in heaven, **John 14:1 – 6**. Jesus is not just preparing a place for His disciples; but He is preparing a special place in heaven for all who would believe in Him as well.

> **John 3:16**: *"For God so loved the world that He gave His only begotten Son, that whoever believes in Him should not perish but have everlasting life."* **NKJV**

It is now the time for God to take the life of Moses for his disobedience of striking the rock. God has Moses to go to the top of Mount Abarim to see the land that He was going to give the children of Israel; and having seen the land, God would then take him to heaven. **Verses 12 & 13**.

Moses asks God for permission to pass on the role of leadership to Joshua before all the people, that there would be less cause for rebellion among the people. **Verses 15 – 17**.

God grants Moses his request, and Joshua is given the blessing of Moses and is inaugurated as the God-chosen leader of Israel before the people. **Verses 18 – 23**.

Again, God leaves nothing undone. He does all things well.

Chapter 28

Offerings

Moses is now 120 years old, and he will soon be taken by God and his earthly life will end; but before he leaves to go upon the mountain, he goes through the requirements for making offerings to the Lord one more time. God desires for all things to be done in order and at the proper time. Never allow your worship of God to be done haphazardly and without forethought. Always give God your very best and serve and worship Him with excellence. God is a God of order, not chaos.

These procedures for <u>Daily Offerings</u>, <u>Sabbath Offerings</u>, <u>Monthly Offerings</u>, <u>Passover Offerings</u> and the <u>Feast of Weeks Offerings</u> are also recorded in **Exodus 29:38 – 46** and **Leviticus 23:5 – 25.** The procedures and requirements for the <u>Feast of Trumpets</u>, the <u>Day of Atonement</u>, and the <u>Feast of Tabernacles</u> listed in the next chapter, **Numbers 29**, are also listed in **Leviticus 23:26 – 44**.

The procedures are detailed and there is to be great care in making all these offerings.

There are some choruses that we enjoy singing regarding the believer's attitude in the worship of God and the lifting up of our vocal offerings to the Lord, such as offerings of praise:

"We bring the sacrifice of praise into the house of the Lord;

We bring the sacrifice of praise into the house of the Lord.

And we offer up to You, the sacrifice of thanksgiving;

And we offer up to You the sacrifice of joy."

Kirk C. Dearman

"Lord, prepare me to be a sanctuary,

Pure and holy, tried and true.

With thanksgiving, I'll be a living sanctuary for You."

John Thompson & Randy Scruggs

We read in Scripture that it is better to give than to receive. Now, receiving does bring joy, but there is greater joy when you give to others. Paul writes in **Acts 20:35**: *"I have shown you in every way, by laboring like this, that you must support the weak. And remember the words of the Lord Jesus, that He said, 'It is more blessed to give than to receive.' "* **NKJV**.

Have you ever been the recipient of a <u>random act of kindness?</u> Do you know what a random act of kindness is? A random act of kindness is some unexpected act of blessing that one believer does for someone that he does not know, and the receiver has no idea as to who the giver is.

Now being a receiver of such a deed brings about great joy, but the person who delivers such a deed receives even greater joy.

Try this out! Do a random act of kindness for some unexpected person, and do not let him or her know your identity. However, God knows and what you do in secret for someone else, God will reward you openly. **Matthew 6:3 & 4**: *"But when you do a charitable deed, do not let your left hand know what your right hand is doing, that your charitable deed may be in secret; and your Father who sees in secret will Himself reward you openly."* **NKJV**

Chapter 29

More Offerings

As Moses continues instructing the people with the remaining offerings or sacrifices, he strictly instructs them in the importance of being holy, righteous, and thorough with God's instructions as they offer them.

He continues with The Feast of Trumpets, also covered in **Leviticus 23:23 – 25,** The Day of Atonement, covered in **Leviticus 23:26 – 32**, and The Feast of Tabernacles, covered in **Leviticus 23:33 – 44**.

With all these offerings they are to include whatever they have vowed to The Lord as a free will offerings. Moses did not leave anything undone, and he did not add anything to what God had told him to instruct the people.

Serving the Lord will cost something. Yes, forgiveness is freely given by God for our confessed sins, and yes, salvation is free to all who would believe; but living a life for the Lord will bring every believer trouble, persecution, and will demand sacrifice. But in all the trouble, persecution, and sacrifice in this world comes God's gift of eternal life.

What happens in this world is but for a moment. The blessings of heaven are eternal.

Remember the words of Missionary Jim Elliott: *"He is no fool who gives what he cannot keep to gain what he cannot lose."* Give of your best to the Master!

Chapter 30

Vows

There is a great responsibility that God requires of fathers and husbands. God is a God of order. We know that there is order in the Godhead, there is order in the family, and there is order in the church. The Apostle Paul addresses this subject in many of his letters: **1 Corinthians 12:12 – 31, Ephesians 5:15 – 6:9, Colossians 3:18 – 25**.

Scripture tells us that to whom much is given, much is required. **Luke 12:48**. Fathers and husbands have been given much responsibility by God and they are to be watchful and quick to act when they see error.

What we see here are rash vows that have been made, specifically by daughters and wives. There is a responsibility that fathers have and husbands.

The responsibility here for fathers and husbands is: While the father is in the house, *"If you hear something, say something,"* **Verse 5**. If the daughter has acted rashly, the father can *overrule her*: *"But _if her father opposes her on the day that he hears of it_, no vow of hers, _no pledge by which she has bound herself shall stand_. And _the Lord will forgive her because her father opposed her._"* **ESV**. The words, *"opposed her"* means that the father would not allow his daughter to fulfill her rash vow. Why would the father not allow her to fulfill the vow?   It is because the daughter has acted rashly and without clear thought.

It is the role of the father to listen to his children, to guide his children in the right, and to protect them when they act unreasonable and unrighteous. The father should be the spiritual leader and priest of his home. Paul writes of the leadership in the home in several places, such as in **Ephesians 5:22 – 6:4**, and **Colossians 3:16 – 22**.

The same process is true with a wife. If her husband hears her speak a rash vow that would bind her, if she says this in the hearing of her husband, the husband can overrule that binding vow before God, and God will honor the objection of her husband. **Verses 6 – 12**.

All vows, oaths, and pledges made to the Lord are binding. **Verse 13**. They are serious things. The only exception is when a father or husband intervenes. If the father or husband does not intervene in that rash vow, then the vow remains binding.

The truth here is to never make a pledge, take an oath, or make a vow that you do not intend to fulfill. Not to fulfill any of these is a sin.

The best thing is to let your "yes" be "yes" and your "no" be "no." Your word should be your bond. It should be the only needed security. **Matthew 5:37**.

All children need to be taught. Children learn more from what they see their parents do than from any book or classroom. What they see their parents do, they will always remember, either good or bad. Therefore, never be known as a grumbler; be known as an encourager. Never be seen by others as a possessor, but as a giver. Never be seen as uncaring, but rather as compassionate. Children are always watching and listening, so live your life to be seen by your children and your wife as a loving and good man of God, who is deeply concerned for his family. There are good and godly fathers and husbands, and there are bad and evil fathers and husbands. Blessed is the family that has a good one!

Now, let me say this about training: I feel that all parents and grandparents should be careful with whom they give consent with the minds of their children. Teachers are not good because they are teachers. Teachers teach what they have been taught and what they believe. If a teacher does not believe in God, he or she will not teach your child to believe in God. If a teacher does not love the country in which you live, they will teach your child not to love your country. If a teacher has been trained in a tyrannical institution, they will train your child to be tyrannical. Be picky about where you place your children to be trained. Here is the truth: Teachers and educators must meet the stringent requirements of parents in order to be given the right to teach their children. No teacher deserves trust just because he or she is a teacher. Teachers must earn the trust of parents in order to be given the privilege to teach their children.

Now having said this, the good teacher who has met the requirements of the parents is a great blessing and is worthy of great praise.

Chapter 31

Revenge on the Midianites

In this chapter we witness the awesome, fearful, and unrelenting vengeance of God being unleashed upon the Midianites, Moabites, and Balaam for vile actions against God's children. It is difficult for one to read this chapter and understand the death and destruction within it. War is violent, extreme, and ruthless. There is no compassionate war. The lesson here for believers is to not be closely involved with people of vile character. Now, these Midianites and Moabites, as well as Balaam, were people of influence but they used their influence to bring about sin. Though it is true that bad people can do good things at times, the reason they are characterized as bad is because they *are* bad.

Believers are told to watch for and resist the devil in their lives in **1 Peter 5:8 & James 4:7 – 9**, but how is that resistance achieved? It is achieved by drawing near to God. God is light and Satan is darkness; and where God is, darkness cannot be. **1 John 1:5**.

If there are things in your life that influence you to do wrong things, get rid of those things and seek the good things. This is what Israel should have done; but they did not; and because they did not, they were influenced by these bad people to commit fornication.

In the battle, Israel kills the five kings of Midian as well as Balaam who was among them. **Verse 8**, *"They killed the kings of Midian with the rest of their slain, Evi, Rekem, Zur, Hur, and*

Reba, the five kings of Midian. And they also killed Balaam the son of Beor with the sword." **ESV**

The last we heard of Balaam was that he had returned to Mesopotamia, but at this time he was back, perhaps collecting pay from the kings for various deeds that he had performed.

The army of Israel is 12,000 strong, 1,000 men from each of the twelve tribes. The battle is quick, and carried out with a great vengeance. Scripture warns: *"It is a fearful thing to fall into the hands of the living God,"* as we read in **Hebrews 10:31 NKJV**.

As the soldiers returned, they had kept alive many of the women. This was not what God had demanded. He demanded all to be killed. We read in **Verses 14 – 18** that the decision of the soldiers not to kill these women angered Moses. Because the soldiers were commanded to carry out the judgment of God which He had decreed to be taken upon them, they were to be killed. Moses points out that these women were among those who had listened to the counsel of Balaam and because of their deeds, a great plague came upon the children earlier.

The booty of war was:

674,000 sheep (337,500 to the fighting men, and 675 to the Lord); **72,000 cattle**, (36,000 to the fighting men, and 72 to the Lord); **61,000 donkeys**, (30,500 to the fighting men and 61 to the Lord); **32,000 young girls** (16,000 to the fighting men and 32 to the Lord), **Verses 32 – 47**. The Levites' portion was set at 1 in every 50 of each. **Verse 47**.

The judgment of God was as follows: *"Now therefore, kill every male among the little ones, and kill every woman who has known man by lying with him. But all the young girls who have not known man by lying with him keep alive for yourselves."* **Verses 17 & 18 ESV**. This is a hard punishment, and this same punishment would be ordered by God in many of the nations and people that Israel would war against in the taking of the Promised Land.

The ways of God are not as the ways of man. There is purpose in all that God does, and with all of this God would work out something good.

In the battle not one Israeli soldier was killed. **Verses 48 & 49**. However, the wrath of God was a fearsome thing as it was unleashed upon the Midianites, Moabites, and Balaam for their sin.

As the 12,000 solders returned from battle, they had to be washed outside the camp and quarantined for seven days because of their having touched dead bodies. All the clothing had to be washed as well. All the gold, silver, copper, lead, and bronze that was taken had to be purified by fire and then water outside the camp. **Verses 21 – 24**.

When preparing for battle, the believer is instructed:

- Put on the armor of God and faithfully stand. **Ephesians 6:10 – 20**

- Resist the devil and draw near God. **James 4:7 – 9**

- Renew and conform your mind to God's thinking. **Romans 12:1 & 2**

- Cleanse their hands, and put away all bitterness. **Ephesians 4:31 & 32 & James 4:8 – 9**

- Walk in the fruit of the Spirit. **Galatians 5:22 – 25**

- Strengthen their faith. **2 Peter 1:5**

When all is said and done, the believer is to continually grow in grace, mercy, and the love of God. And in at all times, remember that the battle belongs to the Lord.

Chapter 32

The Settlement East of Jordan

As the children of Israel are about to take possession of the Promised Land, Moses is approached by the tribes of Reuben and Gad. The tribes of Reuben and Gad are herdsmen and they like what they see in the land east of the Jordan River; it is perfect for raising cattle. What they suggest, at first angers Moses and causes him great concern. Moses expresses his concern to the leaders of Reuben and Gad in **Verses 6 – 30**: *". . . Shall your brethren go to war <u>while you sit here</u>? Now <u>why will you discourage the heart of the children of Israel</u> from going over into the land which the Lord has given them?"* **NKJV**.

What is happening here is that Moses *"prejudges"* the intentions of Reuben, Gad, and half the clan of Manasseh. Moses thinks wrongly that these two and a half tribes are about to abandon the conquest of the Promised Land, just as what had happened in Kadesh Barnea. **Verses 7 – 15**: *"... Thus your fathers did when I sent them away from Kadesh Barnea to see the land. . . . So the Lord's anger was aroused on that day, and He swore an oath, saying, 'Surely none of the men who came up from Egypt, for twenty years old and above, shall see the land of which I swore to Abraham, Isaac, and Jacob, <u>because they have not wholly followed me, except Caleb the son of Jephunneh . . . and Joshua the son of Nun</u>, for they have wholly followed the Lord.' So the Lord's anger was aroused against Israel, and He made them wander in the wilderness forty years, until all the generation that had done evil in the sight of the Lord was gone. <u>And look! You have risen in your father's place, a brood of sinful</u>*

I find it so easy to misjudge people. Don't be too quick to make a judgment upon people. I think this is a besetting sin of my own that I have to continually battle.

The two and a half tribes then assure Moses and the rest of the children of Israel that this is not their intent. They intend to be counted in the battle with them in the conquest of the Promised Land. They only mean that the land east of the Jordan is perfect for raising cattle. **Verses 16 – 19**. Moses is relieved, but he gives them a stern warning as to what God would do to them if they do not make good their promise, **Verses 20 – 27.** *"But if you do not do so, then take note, <u>you have sinned against the Lord; and be sure your sin will find you out.</u>"* **Verse 23**. . . . *If the children of Gad and the children of Reuben cross over the Jordan with you, every man armed for battle before the Lord, and the land is subdued before you, <u>then you shall give them the land of Gilead as a possession</u>. . . . <u>Then the children of Gad and the children of Reuben answered, saying: 'As the Lord has said to your servants, so we will do</u>. . . ."* **Verses 29 – 31 NKJV**.

Chapter 33

A Review of the Wanderings

The situation with Reuben, Gad, and half of Manasseh presents to Moses, who is about to die, the opportunity to review with the children of Israel just what has happened to them as they wandered in the wilderness those forty years. He goes through their encampments and what happened there in **Verses 5 – 50**:

After leaving Rameses the Israelites set up camp at Succoth.

From Succoth they traveled to Etham and set up camp.

From Etham they traveled to Migdol and set up camp.

From Migdol they crossed the Red Sea and then traveled three days to Marah where they set up camp.

From Marah they traveled to the Wilderness of Sin along the Red Sea and camped there.

From the Wilderness of Sin they traveled to Dophkah and set up camp.

From Dophkah they traveled to Rephidim, where they were in dire need of water and God supplied it, and they set up camp.

From Rephidim they traveled to Sinai and set up camp.

From Sinai they traveled to Kibroth-hattaavah and set up camp.

From Kibroth-hattaavah they traveled Hazeroth and set up camp.

From Hazeroth they traveled to Rithmah and set up camp.

From Rithmah they traveled to Rimmon-perez and set up camp.

From Rimmon-perez they traveled to Libnah and set up camp.

From Libnah they traveled to Rissah and set up camp.

From Rissah they traveled to Kehelathah and set up camp.

From Kehelathah they traveled to Mount Shepher and set up camp.

From Mount Shepher they traveled to Haradah and set up camp.

From Haradah they traveled to Makheloth and set up camp.

From Makheloth they traveled to Tahath and set up camp.

From Tahath they traveled to Terah and set up camp.

From Terah they traveled to Mithkah and set up camp.

From Mithkah they traveled to Hashmonah and set up camp.

From Hashmonah they traveled to Moseroth and set up camp.

From Moseroth they traveled to Bene Jaakan and set up camp.

From Bene Jaakan they traveled to Hor Hagidgad and set up camp.

From Hor Hagidgad they traveled to Jotbathah and set up camp.

From Jotbathah they traveled to Abronah and set up camp.

From Abronah they traveled to Ezion Geber and set up camp.

From Ezion Geber they traveled to Kadesh in the Wilderness of Zin and set up camp.

From Kadesh they traveled to Mount Hor, at the border of Edom, and set up camp where Aaron died being 123 years old; and it marked the 40th year of wandering for Israel.

From Mount Hor they traveled to Zalmonah and set up camp.

From Zalmonah they traveled to Punon and set up camp.

From Punon they traveled to Oboth and set up camp.

From Oboth they traveled to Iye-abarim on the border of Moab and set up camp.

From Iye-abarim they traveled to Dibon-gad and set up camp.

From Dibon-gad they traveled to Almon-diblathaim and set up camp.

From Almon-diblathaim they traveled to Mount Nebo and set up camp.

From Mount Nebo they traveled to the plains of Moab by the Jordan River at Beth-jeshimoth, where they were now encamped and ready to cross over into the Promised Land.

In these 40 years there were many sins and there was much complaining. There were wars, and they experienced many plagues and the wrath of God for disobedience, but now it was a new day.

The command from God now is:

- You must drive all the people out. **Verse 52**

- You must destroy all the idols and idol worshippers of the land. **Verse 52**

- You must take possession of all the land. **Verse 53**

- You must settle the land for yourselves. **Verse 53**

Failure to obey all that God has commanded would bring about great judgment. **Verses 55 & 56:** *But if you do not drive out the inhabitants of the land from before you, then those of them whom you let remain shall be as barbs in your eyes and thorns in your sides, and they shall trouble you in the land where you dwell. And I will do to you as I thought to do to them."* **ESV**

Chapter 34

The Boundaries of Canaan

We now see God making known to the children of Israel the boundaries of the Promised Land; and God also makes known the "God selected" and "God approved" leaders. Note this: God is a God of order. He sets boundaries, and He selects those who are to be His godly leaders. From His chosen and called leaders, He demands from his servants godly actions and total obedience.

The children of Israel are at the brink of entering the Promised Land that God had promised them. They had now spent 40 years unnecessarily wandering in their trek to that Promised Land.

On the journey, God led the children of Israel to Sinai, where He gave them His Ten Commandments, the Law, the plans for the priesthood, the Tabernacle of worship, and then He brought them to Kadesh Barnea (**Numbers 14**).

At Kadesh Barnea they committed great sin by their unwillingness to go into the Promised Land and to possess it; all this took two years. **Numbers 14:26 – 38**. God's judgment upon them was that all those who were 20 years old and above would die the wilderness, and their children who were under 20 years of age would inherit the Promised Land.

Now it is 40 years later and they are in Moab, at the Jordan River across from Jericho. And it is here that God gives to them their orders, or their rules of engagement.

Reuben, Gad, and half the tribe of Manasseh, who were given the land east of the Jordan, are reminded of their commitment to fight with their kindred as they do battle in the conquest of the Promised Land.

The borders of the Promised Land are:

- Kadesh Barnea from the south
- Azmon, at the Mediterranean Sea in the south west.
- Mediterranean Sea in the north west to Mount Hor in the east.
- Syria in the north.
- Golan Heights, down the Jordan River to the Dead Sea on the east.
- Reuben, Gad and half of the tribe of Manasseh were given the land east of the Jordan.

God also appoints His approved leaders of each tribe:

- Judah: Caleb son of Jephunneh.
- Simeon: Shemuel son of Ammihud.
- Benjamin: Elidad son of Chislon.
- Dan: Bukki son of Jogli.
- Manasseh: Hanniel son of Ephod.
- Ephraim: Kemuel son of Shiphtan.
- Zebulun: Eliazphan son of Parnach.
- Issachar: Paltiel son of Azzan.
- Asher: Ahihud son of Shelomi.
- Naphtali: Pedahel son of Ammihud.

Joshua has already been appointed by God as the successor of Moses. **Numbers 27:13 – 23**. The rules of engagement by the command of God for the most part would be total annihilation. It was the judgment of God upon those people.

Chapter 35

The Cities of the Levites

The Levites were the priestly tribe of the children of Israel and they would not share in the division of the land. However, they were given 48 cities in which to live and the land that surrounded them for the raising of cattle.

Of those 48 cities, there were appointed 6 that would be cities of refuge, or I could say sanctuary cities. These cities were for those who had killed someone accidentally or unintentionally; the term used here is *"manslayer,"* **Verse 11 NKJV**, which our laws refer to as manslaughter.

There were three cities of refuge on the west side of the Jordan and three cities on the east side of the Jordan. **Joshua 20** lists them:

On the west side of the Jordan River:

1. **Kedesh** in Galilee, **Verse 7**
2. **Shechem** in Ephraim, **Verse 7**
3. **Kirjath Arba** (Hebron) in Judah, **Verse 7**

On the "other side of the Jordan" or the east side:

1. **Bezer** of Reuben, **Verse 8**
2. **Ramoth** of Gad in Gilead, **Verse 8**
3. **Golan** of Manasseh in Bashan, **Verse 8**

The 48 cities given to the Levites are listed in **Joshua 21**:

1. The **Kohathite** Clan in the tribe of Levi who were direct descendants of Aaron: <u>13 towns</u> from the tribes of Judah, Simeon, and Benjamin. **Joshua 21:4**
2. The **remainder of the Kohathite** Clan: <u>10 towns</u> of the tribes of Ephraim, Dan and half-tribe of Manasseh, **Joshua 21:5**
3. The Clan of **Gershon:** <u>13 towns</u> from the tribes of Issachar, Asher, Naphtali and half of Manasseh, **Joshua 21:6.**
4. The Clan of **Merari**: <u>12 towns</u> from the tribes of Reuben, Gad and Zebulun, **Joshua 21:7.**

The reason for the six cities of refuge was that they were to be places of refuge from any avenger for his unintentional crime. *"When you cross the Jordan into the land of Canaan, then <u>you shall select cities to be cities of refuge for you, that the manslayer who kills any person without intent may flee there. The cities shall be for you a refuge from the avenger, that the manslayer may not die until he stands before the congregation for judgment.</u> And the cities that you give shall be your six cities of refuge. You shall give three cities beyond the Jordan, and three cities in the land of Canaan, to be cities of refuge. These six cities shall be for refuge for the people of Israel, and for the stranger and for the sojourner among them, that anyone who kills any person without intent may flee there. "But if he struck him down with an iron object, so that he died, he is a murderer. The murderer shall be put to death."* **Verses 10 – 16 ESV.**

Life is precious to God, for He is the creator of all life, and life begins at conception. Notice what Moses writes regarding the life of the preborn baby in Exodus: **Exodus 21:22**, *"If men fight, and hurt a woman with child, so that she gives birth prematurely, yet no harm follows, he shall surely be punished accordingly as the woman's husband imposes on him: and he shall pay as the judges determine.* **NKJV.**

An adult is a person, a child is a person, an elderly adult is a person, and a fetus is a person. To intentionally cause the death any person, including a preborn child, is as much of a murder as causing the death of a visible child. Scripture tells us that life is in the blood. *"For the life of the flesh is in the blood, and I have given it to you upon the altar to make atonement for your souls; for it is the blood that makes atonement for the soul."* **Leviticus 17:11 NKJV**. Whatever has flowing blood has life.

Until the time of trial, that *"manslayer"* is kept safe as long as he or she is in that city of refuge. **Verse 26**. Judgment will be made at the trial, or he will be freed when the high priest that was living at the time of his or her crime dies. **Verse 25**.

The sentence for murder is death, but the sentence of death cannot be made upon the accusation of one person. There must be at least two witnesses. *"Whoever kills a person, the murder shall be put to death on the <u>testimony of witnesses; but one witness is not sufficient testimony against a person for the death penalty"</u>.* **Verse 30 NKJV**.

When intentional or premeditated murder is proven, that person must be put to death quickly. **Verses 16 & 30**.

The chapter concludes with the preciousness of blood. Blood that is shed and falls upon the land is precious blood: *"Therefore do not defile the land which you inhabit, in the midst of which I dwell; for I, the Lord dwell among the children of Israel."* **Verse 34 NKJV**.

The most precious blood of all is the blood of Jesus that was shed for the sin of the world. The hymn "Nothing But the Blood," written by Robert Lowery, expresses this preciousness of the blood of Jesus:

Nothing But The Blood

What can wash away my sin?

Nothing but the blood of Jesus;

What can make me whole again?

Nothing but the blood of Jesus.

O precious is the flow,

That makes me white as snow.

No other fount I know;

Nothing but the blood of Jesus."

Robert Lowery

Chapter 36

Female Heirs

In **Chapter 27** Mahlah, Noah, Hoglah, Milcah, and Tirzah, the five daughters of Zelophehad, who was the great, great, great, great, great grandson of Joseph through the lineage of his son Manasseh, came before Moses pleading for an inheritance of land. Because they did not have children, they did not have the right to inherit land. As they brought before Moses their plea, God confirmed to Moses that the plea of the five women was just and right, so Moses promised them a possession of land to inherit. *"And the Lord spoke to Moses, saying: 'The daughters of Zelophehad speak what is right; you shall surely give them a possession of inheritance among their father's brothers, and cause the inheritance of their father to pass to them.'"* **Numbers 27:6 & 7 NKJV**.

The daughters now remind Moses of the command of God and Moses makes good on his promise to the five women. *"Just as the Lord commanded Moses, so did the daughters of Zelophehad; for Mahlah, Tirzah, Hoglah, Milcah, and Noah, the daughters of Zelophehad, were married to the sons of their father's brothers. They were married into the families of the children of Manasseh the son of Joseph, and their inheritance remained in the tribe of their father's family."* **Verses 10 – 12 NKJV**.

The book of Numbers ends with a confirmation of its authenticity: *"These are the commandments and the rules that the Lord commanded through Moses to the people of Israel in the plains of Moab by the Jordan at Jericho."* **Verse 13 ESV**.

The final truth that is brought forth here is that every person ought to be a person of worth, a person of trust, a person of his word, and a faithful follower of Christ Jesus.

There were many bad things that happened to the children of Israel. With those bad things, bad choices were made and some good choices were made.

We live in a bad world, so expect bad things to happen, but when they do happen, make the right choice.

Having said that, let me say this: When you pray, don't ask God to keep you from bad things. Ask Him to keep you from choosing evil things. This world is bad, and bad things are going to happen to good people. However, in the bad things choose to do good things.

When you pray, ask God to keep others from evil and from choosing evil things.

Don't be bitter; don't be known as an angry person.

Don't be wrathful, but gracious and merciful.

Don't be covetous of things that others have; give from what you have to others.

Don't judge others; be an encourager of others.

Don't hate anyone; show the love of God to everyone.